SEVEN DEADLY SINS OF MANAGEMENT

Tim

Enjoy the read

IHW.

Quo Vadis Publications Ltd

Cirrus Building
6 International Avenue
ABZ Business Park
Dyce Drive
Aberdeen
AB21 0BH

T: +44 224 920037

vic@quovadispublications.com

www.quovadispublications.com

Quo Vadis Publications Ltd
Cirrus Building, 6 International Avenue,
ABZ Business Park, Dyce Drive
Aberdeen, Scotland
AB21 0BH
Tel: (+44) 1224 920037
Email: vic@quovadispublications.com
Web: www.quovadispublications.com

ISBN 978-1-326-97052-9

British Library Cataloguing in Publication Data.

A catalogue record for this book is available from the British
Library.

Printed and bound in the USA by Lulu Press, Inc. 627 David
Drive, Suite 300, Morrisville, NC 27560

Quo Vadis Publications Ltd is an imprint of Lulu Press Inc

This book explores some of the behavioural characteristics in management that can lead to sub-optimal financial performance and undermine both reputation and shareholder value.

Ian Campbell argues that these behavioural characteristics fall into two categories.

The first category consists of those characteristics that are a positive force when exercised in moderation but become damaging when they are used to excess or become uncontrolled. The second category consists of those characteristics that are damaging at any level.

Ian supports his contentions using well publicised and high profile corporate events alongside personal insights and experiences from an interesting and varied career. The book offers food for thought for shareholders, both large and small, and for the managers who perpetrate the seven deadly sins.

Contents

Foreword by Henry Ellington

Ian Campbell has written a book that may well become one of the classics of management education, a book that should be studied and used in all good business schools. Why do I make such a claim? Because Ian has shown how the basic Popperian principle of 'error elimination' can be applied to the work of managers, thus enabling them to become **good** managers by identifying –and eliminating– some of the most harmful and destructive characteristics of **bad** managers.

In 1934, the Austrian philosopher Karl Popper wrote a book on the scientific method that revolutionised the way in which we view science, and later applied his basic methodology to other areas, including politics. Indeed, his work provided many of the theoretical foundations for modern social democracy. In 1984, my colleague Fred Percival and I applied his basic ideas to course and curriculum development. Ian Campbell has now done the same thing for the practice of management.

I was extremely flattered to be asked to write the 'Foreword' to this excellent, exciting and extremely helpful book. I wish it all the success it deserves.

Emeritus Professor Henry Ellington

Chairman and Founding Author

Quo Vadis Publications Ltd.

Acknowledgements

Specific quotes from business writers, business leaders and others are acknowledged in the text of my book. Quotes from meetings or discussions have all been made from memory and are therefore not specifically attributed or acknowledged. Where I have quoted things that were said, I have done so as accurately as I can based on my memory of events but I have not named sources in case I have misquoted.

I want to thank all the people I have worked with over the years. You all contributed to making my working life an interesting, enjoyable and varied experience. Some of you I got along well with and some less so but all your contributions were positive.

Special thanks go to my partner Kate for all her encouragement, support and critique as well as for her proof-reading and editing duties.

Ian Campbell

Authors' Introduction and Background

After almost thirty years spent (in the most part successfully) in senior financial roles in an assortment of different companies and a number of different countries, I felt well qualified to be writing a book about management. Following a two-year career break during which the book was first drafted, I went on to enjoy six years in financial management and general management in the public sector where I witnessed many of the same value-destroying behaviours that I had seen in industry and a style of management that I thought I had left behind in the nineteen-seventies. I wanted to incorporate some of this public sector experience into my book but knitting it elegantly into the draft, which was based on business and shareholder value, was too much of a challenge for me. The easy way out was to add a separate chapter on the public sector and that is what I have done.

Firstly, let me give you some more detailed credentials.

I am a Chartered Accountant who moved into industry shortly after qualifying and then stayed there. For reasons that made sense to a newly turned twenty-two year old at the time, I had decided that the profession wasn't where I wanted to be and it's a decision that I never had cause to regret or revisit. My early career was somewhat unstructured and I had two or three fairly short stops before settling down. Thereafter I made a lot more moves but they were predominantly moves within the same company rather than moves between companies. With only a couple of exceptions, the moves were at the instigation of my employer and were either promotional or lateral across international borders. I look back positively at all of the moves that I made, and my working life has always been challenging, interesting and rewarding. During this 'first career', I lived and worked in six different countries and carried out work assignments in around thirty others. My direct bosses included several Americans, an Austrian, an Egyptian and, of course, some obligatory Brits (Scots, English and Irish but never a Welshman).

To illustrate the kind of variation I have seen in management styles, I had one American boss who nurtured (and worked on) the ambition to reduce his direct reports to an absolute essential minimum. When he moved on, his successor (who was also American) seemed hell bent on going in the opposite direction and the senior management team quickly grew from the boss plus six or seven direct reports to the boss plus fifteen direct reports. It was the same business, same size and similar organisational structure but we saw two entirely different philosophies on how it should be run. The first of these bosses liked to think of himself as a strategist, who saw his role as a one-man think-tank evolving the master plan for the business while the on-going chores of day-to-day management were being taken care of around him. The second was a much more accomplished leader who was effective at both the strategic and detailed levels. He did, however, have one significant weakness which was that he had a big slice of the control-freak in him. Superficially he was open and sharing but he shared different pieces of the puzzle with different people and there were always a few pieces that he kept strictly to himself. It seems likely that it was this need to control that drove him to try to work with such a big management team.

Another illustration of the fundamental difference in the management styles of these two individuals is that the first one would happily have lived without an annual budgeting exercise (if it hadn't been demanded from above) and he kept himself on the periphery of the whole budget process. By contrast, the second one spent hours playing with numbers and 'gaming' the budget at a detailed level to try to ensure that we got away with a set of targets that he was comfortable with. As you may imagine, the change was quite a culture shock for the organisation in general and, more particularly, for the managers who had worked on both these gentlemen's management teams, including me.

At a peer level I worked alongside managers from thirty or forty different countries. I worked in big companies, small companies, small autonomous units within large groups, geographically structured organisations, functionally structured organisations, product based organisations, hybrid organisations, matrix organisations, hierarchical organisations and flat organisations. I directly managed business restructuring, cost-reduction programmes, business mergers, business integration, business disposals, a business start-up, due-diligence exercises and IT implementation and enhancement programmes (big and small). Then, to round it all off, I had the eye-opener that was the public sector.

Over the years I have worked in, around and under a lot of different cultures and a lot of different styles but the biggest influences on me, from a business point of view, have undoubtedly been American. Oh yes indeed, America, the home of the brave and land of the free, where everything is bigger, including most of the seven sins that are the subject of this book!

The Americans have made a whole industry out of the promulgation and promotion of management theory and I have lived successively (and successfully) through Total Quality Management, Just-in-Time Production, Business Process Re-engineering, Constraints Management, Activity Based Management and Six-Sigma. Unsurprisingly, there was not one of these that proved to be the panacea that it had been hyped up to be, although each undoubtedly resulted in some level of net benefit for the business.

I have read my share of Goldratt, Hargrove, Whitney, Waitley, Collins, Peters, Porras, Deming, Kaplan and others. It's interesting to see how, as one business 'guru' fades from fashion, another rises to take his or her place. A few, like Deming, endure but most have their few years of glory and then presumably settle into the college lectures and after-dinner speech tour. When you have read a few of these 'experts', you soon realise how little there really is in the way of new and radical ideas. Most of the 'new' insights are simply the development of old themes or old themes dressed in new clothes.

When radical ideas do occasionally come forward, they tend to be theoretical (rather than practical) and to be technically complex. So much so, that they either remain little more than an idea or, like Kaplan's Activity Based Costing and Balanced Scorecard, their success is reflected in a relatively short and steep-sided temporal bell-curve.

Although they are repackaged and have had some bells and whistles added, you will find that golden oldies such as 'continuous improvement' and 'right first time' are still at the core of many doctrines. The constant repackaging keeps the consultants gainfully employed, which is good for their wallets and the employment statistics but probably for little else. In my view, 'continuous improvement' and 'right first time' are both concepts that need no reinvention. I fully subscribe to both and have always tried to work to them. They have precisely the right ingredients to be successful and enduring management tools because they are logical, conceptually simple and easily understood by staff at all levels of the organisation.

I liken 'continuous improvement' to having a steel chain. Find the weakest link, replace it or strengthen it and then start looking for the next weakest link. When you find it, replace or strengthen it and go after the next one. If you continuously hunt down the weakest link in your chain and strengthen it or replace it with one that is stronger, your whole chain will always be getting stronger. It will also be stronger than that of someone who started with a similar chain but who has made no improvements, or that of someone who has only made spasmodic improvements to their chain. The analogous 'links' for this purpose can be people, systems, processes or any other component that contributes to the operation of the business. This sounds simple but applying it in reality requires a crossing the Rubicon for many managers. Simply recognising that there is room for improvement and accepting that the status quo isn't going to deliver the bacon in an ever-increasingly competitive world are still 'lights on' events for far too many managers. Asking them to address this on a one-time basis is a challenge. Getting them to accept it as part of their ethos and day-to-day thought processes is getting into loaves and fishes territory. Nowhere, I have discovered, is this more pertinent than in the public sector.

Once in a while there will be a competitor out there who, through technical innovation or other nefarious means, comes up with a chain that is made of a higher-grade material or a substantially cheaper material than yours and then you, in turn, will need to come up with some step-change improvement or be left floundering in the distance. In most cases, though, a focussed and on-going programme of continuous improvement will keep your company well towards the head of the competitive pack. It's analogous to R & D where Research is looking for step-change and Development is the continuous effort to stay up with and ahead of the game.

In the same vein, imagine if everything that everybody did in your business was done correctly at the first time of asking. Inspection and checking would become redundant and probably a quarter to a half of most people's time would become free. It's a staggering statistic but that's the kind of proportion of total time that is being spent by Mr or Mrs Average Employee in checking and correcting their own work and the work of others. People will always make mistakes, but a few minutes or seconds spent in carefully reviewing your own work, before you release it, can save hours of wasted time and effort further along the process. 'Right first time' is such a simple concept but it's oh so very hard to make it a reality.

Continuous improvement and getting things right first time are both areas where the public-sector lags way behind the private sector. Changing the culture in the National Health Service or in Higher Education to embrace these ideas on a day-to-day basis could, in my opinion, save billions of pounds in bureaucracy and failure costs.

I am also a disciple of Six Sigma but it needs to be approached with caution and with eyes wide-open. Six Sigma is the statistical target of 3.4 defects per one million opportunities. The methodology for driving towards this goal is designed to recreate processes so that defects are never produced in the first place. This highly prescriptive programme offers a scientific approach to achieving step-change improvements in first-pass yield and in driving out defects and has enjoyed some high-profile success stories (GE and Motorola were early adopters). Six Sigma is definitely on the march but be warned that it's a heavyweight programme in terms of both resource commitment and cost and it's not for the uncommitted or the faint-hearted. If you are not going to undertake Six Sigma wholeheartedly then you are better to stay well away from it!

As I neither profess nor aspire to be a business guru or an expert in the theory of business, I won't burden you with any more concepts. What I am (or what I like to think I am) is an experienced and accomplished manager and an interested observer of people. I have a pragmatic and 'can do' style, a strong results-focus, a good commercial brain and I like to finish what I start. An industrial psychologist once told me that I was a person who understood his own shortcomings and who was comfortable with himself. It's a description that I like. Recognising and accepting your own shortcomings is the essential first step in curing them or, at least, in knowing how to manage them.

To avoid having to repeat 'he/she' or 'him/her' every time I use the personal pronoun, I have stuck to the simple 'he' and 'him' to encompass both genders in my book. My sincerest apologies go to all the lady readers who would have preferred the female form to take precedent – Please believe me when I tell you that I gave serious consideration to writing the book that way but, as my fingers approached the key-board, my testosterone just wouldn't let me do it!

My thoughts in this book are based entirely on reality and experience. I have illustrated points by narrating specific personal experiences, wherever possible, but I have deliberately been non-specific regarding names, places and dates to spare any individual embarrassment and, equally importantly, to try to avoid being sued.

We all have our strengths as well as our weaknesses but, in drawing on examples to illustrate the seven sins, I have focussed almost entirely on individual weaknesses (or 'areas for growth and development', to give them their more positive name). In most cases, the individuals who I have used in my examples are people who have a lot of offsetting strengths and, if I ever get around to writing a treatise on the seven virtues of management I will endeavour to use some of the more positive characteristics of these same individuals in my illustrations.

To those who think that they recognise themselves and are unhappy with what they read, I can only shrug my shoulders and say, "If the cap fits, wear it. If the cap doesn't fit, it is obviously not intended to be you".

In writing a book with this particular subject matter, I am in no way trying to imply that I am some sort of paragon of virtue. As you will see in the following chapters, I have been rightly accused of both Arrogance and Bullying in the workplace. On the other hand, Greed, Indecision and Profligacy are sins that I have avoided succumbing to. Nepotism and Cloning is a bit more subjective but I can put my hand on my heart and say that, when recruiting or promoting, my absolute priority has always been to find the best person for the job regardless of their age, sex, ethnic background or the colour of their skin. Of course, if it seemed likely that they would strengthen the Finance department's five-a-side soccer team they got a couple of extra points in my final assessment! When it comes to 'Spin', I have been around plenty of it and I am not so naive to believe I have been untainted by it. However, I have always endeavoured to present business issues in a balanced, meaningful and fair way, regardless of who my audience might be.

Business books can (and often do) make dry and difficult reading so I have tried to break the mould by keeping my subject matter interesting and making this a light and entertaining read. At the same time, the book carries some serious messages and I trust that readers who invest in the equity markets or in private companies will find it encourages them to think in more detail about how the companies that they are invested in are being managed and whether or not they are getting full value from their management and achieving the right return on their investment.

Hopefully you will find some of my specific experiences to be amusing (recollecting them certainly made me smile) but there are serious messages underpinning them all. For managers who read the book, I hope that it will stimulate some thought and perhaps it will cause them to consider some of their own behaviour in a new light. I remember a leadership consultant telling me that, when it comes to inter-personal relationships, perceptions are every bit as important as realities. My experience is that he was absolutely right. So, all you managers and aspiring managers, please pause for a few moments and think about how others may perceive *you*. It will be time well spent.

As the great Scots bard, Robert Burns wrote......

"O wid some power the giftie gie us

To see oorsels as ithers see us."

Enjoy the read!

Chapter 1: What is management and why 'SINS'?

So, what is management and why do I use the word 'sins'?

Let's start with management. The easy answer, of course, is that management means different things to different people. The Chambers 21st Century Dictionary defines it as *'the skill or practice of controlling. Directing or planning something, especially a commercial enterprise or activity'*. However, if I am going to write meaningfully about management, I feel that I need to start by giving it my own definition in the context of this book.

For this purpose, I shall define 'management' the people rather than 'management' the skill. Here it is.....

Management is the generic name given to the people who are employed to strategise, plan, guide, lead and direct an organisation or enterprise, and to make sure that all the enabling assets and resources are in place, to meet the short and long term goals of the organisation's or enterprise's stakeholders.

It obviously follows that the skill of 'management' is the ability to effectively and successfully achieve those responsibilities.

My definition is not a particularly long sentence but it does encompass a very wide range of skills and responsibilities. For example, a key subset of ensuring that all the enabling assets and resources are in place is having the right people in the right jobs. When it comes to people, the manager has to be able to motivate, mentor, develop, guide, assist, support, push, persuade, negotiate and cajole, as well as to organise and lead. Few employees will demand all these skills from their manager on any regular basis but, across the spectrum of all employees, using these skills will be part of the manager's daily routine and he needs to have all the appropriate abilities in his locker.

In his 'action centred leadership' approach, John Adair suggests that three essential elements are required in all leadership situations:

- achieve the task
- manage the team
- manage individuals

This succinct summary provides a simple mantra for all leaders and managers to carry with them to help ground and refocus them when things are not going to plan and work worries are interfering with a good night's sleep.

The organisation's goals will necessarily cover social and environmental responsibilities as well as financial performance but, in the case of quoted companies, the primary goal is, most commonly, for long-term growth in shareholder value. In the case of a public sector body or a mutual company or a co-operative, the goals will be something different (and typically more complex) but in those organisations it is still, in my view, incumbent on the managers to ensure that the stakeholders' goals are achieved as efficiently and as economically as possible.

Most managers in industry are competitively paid for the work that they do and the shareholders have a right to assume that, in return, those managers will be looking after the shareholders' best interests rather than taking care of themselves. Unfortunately, with human nature being what it is, many managers are more focussed on their own self-interest than they are on the greater good of the whole organisation. In outlining the background to the appointment of the Cadbury committee, Alistair Ross Goodbey, the chairman of the International Governance Network, described this type of situation as one 'where the executive rode roughshod over the interests of the outside shareholders'. There is no doubt that a healthy complement of hungry and ambitious people within a business is likely to drive that business forward but the right balance has to be struck between the self-interests of the managers and the interests of the shareholders. It is where and how the balance is struck that defines management's actions as virtue or sin.

How many times have you seen hungry and ambitious people progressively promoted out of their own messes until they reach a level where they fail badly and consequently do some serious damage? You must know the type. Typically they are pushy, they wear their ambition on their sleeve and they have the gift of the gab. They are polished and persuasive in presentations, they shy away from controversial decisions, they pamper to their bosses and they network well. Their most glaring characteristic is that they very rarely finish what they start. In short, they are a triumph of form over substance and they are *not* value-adding contributors to the business. Interestingly (and unsurprisingly) the results of some research into management behaviour have indicated that people who tell lies are the people most likely to succeed. It is a situation that is understandable but wholly undesirable. Filtering these folk out before they reach their level of incompetence is not easy but it's nonetheless galling to see how many of them survive and prosper at senior levels in major corporations.

From the shareholders' perspective, that is a sin. In fact, it has a double 'whammy' for the shareholder because these people are not only potentially damaging to the business but they add little or no value to the organisation and, at a senior level, they are expensive to employ.

It is a simple precept of successful business that every employee has to generate value for the company that exceeds their own total employment costs plus the cost of any materials that they consume or cause to be consumed. Total employment costs obviously have to include an appropriate component for facilities, equipment and other essential infrastructure as well as the obvious direct costs such as salary, payroll taxes, travel, phone calls and stationery. It shouldn't take an accountant or a mathematician to figure out that, if this is not happening, the business is destined for failure. If shareholders' interests are to be properly safeguarded, they need to have managers who are, first and foremost, hungry and ambitious for the successful development of the business and who are comfortable in the knowledge that if they contribute to the success of the business, their own careers and rewards will be assured.

"You must be joking", I hear some of you say. "Trust the company to look after my career advancement – surely you are pulling my chain!"

Well, perhaps I was over-stating the case slightly! The point I am making is that promotion and career progression should be based on deeds and not on unfulfilled promises. However, there can be no doubt that, whatever the scale of your real achievements, it always helps to make sure that you are seen to do a good job by the people who matter. Some carefully directed self-publicity is no bad thing, provided that it is backed up by some real successes and not just the promise of success.

A couple of quotes from Jack Welch, the former Chief Executive Officer (CEO) of GE, provide an excellent summary to this:

- *"At a deeper level, we found that for leaders to make something great, their ambition has to be for the greatness of the work and the company, rather than for themselves."*
- *"We never liked people more focussed on the next job than the one they were doing. This could be a career killer."*

Equally important for your progression, of course, is that you fit with the style and culture of the company and can work comfortably with your bosses and peers. If you have a problem with all, or most, of them it's time for some self-analysis. Someone once said that if, by ten o'clock in the morning, most of the people you have met that day are idiots, then it's time to duck into the toilet and take a good hard look in the mirror. It is an excellent piece of advice.

I can recollect three occasions in my career when I found that I was working within a culture that was alien to me...............

The first situation was when I went to work for one of the Industrial Training Boards back in the early nineteen-seventies. I simply wasn't equipped to handle the 'management by committee' and the lack of any profit motive in the organisation. In Campbell's world, if you see a problem, you scope it and fix it. In the world of the 1970s Industrial Training Boards, if you saw a problem, you wrote a report about it and passed it to a committee where it was presented, analysed and discussed. If the problem was, in any way, a significant one it would be likely to get deferred to the next committee meeting, pending the gathering of additional advice and/or information. Before joining the ITB, I had been interviewed by the man who was to be my boss there (the CFO) and, prior to his position at the ITB, he had spent a lot of years working for a well-known global business that enjoyed a high reputation for the quality of its management. His pedigree and (of course) the attractive salary being offered were the two factors that lured me into the job. Unfortunately it turned out that my boss was so laid-back on a day-to-day basis that the bureaucracy and lack of urgency didn't appear to faze him at all. He rolled with it and didn't let it visibly upset him. Whether he was internally as relaxed is something I can't answer. I could only judge what I could see and the mystery to me was how this man had survived and prospered in his previous role. By contrast, I simply couldn't handle it. I stayed with the ITB for a little less than one year before heading back to the cut-and-thrust of what I regarded as a real job.

My second experience came fifteen years later and was in a supposed culture of equals. All employees were 'associates', all employees were in a share ownership plan and all employees had part of their compensation based on departmental, regional or company-wide performance. There was a core group of senior management who zealously guarded the culture and decided who was a 'fit' and who wasn't. If you didn't fit (or appear to fit), you weren't going to progress. The culture itself was okay but the hypocrisy that existed within that company was unbelievable. It was stupid things like the 'anybody can park anywhere' arrangement reverting to an unofficial (but rigidly enforced) system of allocated parking for the senior managers when the corporate bosses weren't in town. I was a vocal critic of the hypocrisy and quickly had a 'culturally incompatible' label tattooed on my forehead. My boss would tell me privately what a joke he thought it all was, but he had learned to 'play the game' and he was very much a 'golden boy'. With a large dose of Campbell subtlety, my ultimate crime was to ask my boss publicly (with the most deadpan face that I could muster) why the Company Driver wasn't giving my boss's car its usual weekly wash when the CEO was in town. To say he was not amused is a giant understatement. In that environment you either keep your non-conforming views to yourself or you move on. Not being able to shut-up, I moved on after only nine months, by mutual agreement. (They told me that my position was redundant and I agreed!)

The third experience lasted considerably longer and that was my late career venture into the Higher Education sector. I was reintroduced to the management style of the 1970s ITB but on a much bigger scale. This time I lasted much longer but I was older, wiser and more relaxed and I think I perhaps offered a certain novelty value to the Academic hierarchy. However, my time there was always tenuous and I was chastised more than once over the tone and directness of my communication. In terms of the tone and delivery, those chastisements reminded me of being back at school. Not exactly what one expects when one is a Managing Director and passed one's sixtieth birthday!

It's common to find that, within an organisation's broader management structure, there is a small core group or 'inner sanctum' where all the important decisions are in fact made, including those affecting the career progression of individual employees. In his book, 'Who really matters: the core group theory of power, privilege and success', Art Kleiner states that in any organisation there is an all-powerful core group upon which all others' career success depends. In my view this is somewhat of a blanket generalisation, but it does describe a situation that undoubtedly exists in far too many enterprises, in both the private and public sectors. It is also a situation that is likely to have one or more of the seven sins at its root and providing its sustenance. Arrogance, bullying, greed and nepotism/cloning can all result in the evolution of a controlling core group that is intolerant towards anyone who does not fit with its own goals and image.

I came across the controlling core group on a number of occasions in my career. This included one company where the controlling group dressed themselves up in their best bib-and-tucker every Friday evening for their weekly male bonding rituals at the Masonic Lodge! If you weren't a member of the Lodge, your career prospects were severely limited. When I pushed for the office fridge and crockery to be returned from the Lodge, I was informed (with studied sincerity) that I was upsetting some very influential people and that I had been black-balled from every Lodge in West Africa. As it happens, I had no aspirations in that direction. I cannot recall whether the fridge and crockery were recovered but I suspect not! In my second example of 'cultural incompatibility' above there was definitely a small core group at the top of the organisation who controlled people's careers based more on 'cultural fit' than on individual contribution or ability.

As an aside, I remember participating in an excellent Leadership Development Programme where, in one of the sessions, I was paired with one of my peers to go through a mutual 'show-and-tell'. I had five minutes to speak to him about my strengths and weaknesses, and my career achievements, aspirations and frustrations, without any interruptions from him. He then had two or three minutes to give me his views and feedback, with no interruptions from me. Following that we reversed roles. It was a therapeutic and cathartic session and there was one insight that my 'buddy' gave me that I found particularly perceptive and thought provoking. I instantly recognised the trait in myself but I had simply never thought about it as being a problem. "You don't pick your fights carefully enough", he said. "You need to learn to keep your powder dry for the fights that really matter and learn to let the small skirmishes go by you, no matter how tempting it is to go in with all guns blazing."

My preference has always been to hire and work with managers who would challenge me and offer substance above form. Some 'form' (not in the sense used by the criminal justice system) is unquestionably important but there is no substitute for substance when it comes to the success of the organisation over the long-term.

However, as a manager, it can be hard to objectively evaluate people who you have come to rely on or people who have successfully positioned themselves to be close to you. Most difficult of all are the people who you regard as friends. How many managers do you know who work with a small, select 'inner sanctum' consisting of their apparent pals? I say 'apparent' because typically these are the kind of 'friends' who, when the sharks are circling, will swim off at high speed and leave you to your fate. I always tried to work with my whole team and not to single out a few favourites but I must confess that I wasn't always successful.

At one time I had a manager working for me who I thought was just excellent. I'll call him 'Pete', although that wasn't his real name. Pete did whatever I asked of him, was available when I needed him and agreed with me on most things. He and I became quite friendly and he and his teenage son used to regularly play tennis (or our rather primitive version of the game) with my teenage son and me on a Sunday morning. One day I was talking to one of my other direct reports and extolled Pete's virtues to him. I think I said something to the effect of, "If I had a few more as good as Pete working for me, things would be a lot better round here." The person I was talking to screwed up his face disapprovingly, gave an embarrassed laugh and asked me, "How would you know whether Pete's good or not?" I asked him what he meant and he told me. "Well he's so far up your backside that we have to pull him out by the ankles whenever we want to talk to him." We both laughed at his description but it gave me some real food for thought. Six months later, viewing Pete's performance more dispassionately, I still thought that he was a solid and reliable employee but I could see that he wasn't the star I had once thought. He was a perfect 'yes man', who had developed ingratiation into a fine art, and I had failed to pick up on it. Pete and I remained friends but I let the tennis matches lapse and became much more objective in assessing his work performance thereafter. You need to get along with the people that you work with but there is no question that friendships in the workplace can cloud performance judgement no matter how smart the manager is and no matter how convinced he is in his own mind that he can separate the work and social aspects.

Successful managers and leaders are likely to be confident and self-assured by nature. They also need to have a bit of the bully in them to push people when a push is needed and, yes, they will probably be driven by money. These are all virtues from the shareholders' perspective, because they are characteristics that are needed to drive a successful business. Unfortunately though, you can have too much of a good thing.

The Chambers 21st Century Dictionary defines sin, in a non-religious context, as *'an act that offends common standards of morality or decency; an outrage'*. This is quite strong but I like this definition and I am sticking to the word.

The sin comes when confidence and self-assurance manifest themselves as arrogance and a failure to listen to others or when the drive for personal wealth goes over the edge into personal greed. Similarly, the ability to present well and show a not-so-good situation in a favourable light can be desirable when there is a need to be optimistic and upbeat, such as when the audience is a customer, a supplier, the banker or your employees. For example, at a communication meeting with the company's employees you want to be open and honest but you also need to be upbeat and positive about the business. If you stand up and tell the employees that it's all gloom and doom out there, you may as well close the doors immediately because that's the impact you will have. The sin is when spin is deliberately used to hide, or disguise, problems from senior managers or the Board of Directors when they have a right, and a need, to know of the difficulties.

Further up the management ladder, the Board of Directors has a responsibility to be honest with the shareholders and with the investment community. In each of these cases, there is a very fine line to be walked and most managers who cross over that line never get back to the right side. Once you start suppressing reality you will quickly become like the compulsive gambler who is constantly 'robbing Peter to pay Paul' and looking for just one big win to get him out of the ever-growing mess that is piling up behind him.

Other behavioural characteristics such as indecision and profligacy are never a virtue, even in moderation. They are management sins – end of story.

The lines between some of these seven sins are blurred because some behavioural characteristics are spin-offs from, or subsets of, others. For example, bullying can be a by-product of arrogance. Profligacy that benefits the individual is clearly a subset of both arrogance and greed, and so on. The sins are inter-related and sometimes blurred at the edges but they are nonetheless individually identifiable.

Many years ago, when I was working in Internal Audit, I carried out a routine review of one of our Northern European subsidiaries. In terms of both market share and profitability this subsidiary was amongst our best performers within the Europe/Africa Division. The local Managing Director was a charismatic, dynamic and entrepreneurial individual who ran the business as if it was his own, nurturing a family atmosphere that undoubtedly contributed substantially to the subsidiary's excellent results. Unfortunately the MD treated it as his own business to the extent that his wife had a credit card in the company's name and she used it to pay for some of her grocery shopping, all of her petrol and frequent meals with the kids. The MD also managed to structure a deal where he thought he could rationalise and justify getting the car of his choice even though the capital cost was well outside his approved budget. He broke the rules and parted ways with the company but, in this instance, it was not a simple issue of greed or profligacy. The issue was that he thought that the wife's credit-card and the particular model of car were normal 'perks' for the Managing Director of a successful company of the size of the business that he was running. Because the company didn't provide them as a matter of course, he helped himself. The motive for his actions was superficially greed and his behaviour was certainly profligate but his real sin was arrogance! I remember as a lowly Internal Auditor struggling to come to terms with the fact that the company would get rid of one of its most talented managers under these circumstances and it was explained to me that it was necessary as an example to others. The rules, controls and delegated authorisation levels were there for a purpose and had to be adhered to. Making exceptions was the start of a potentially long rocky downhill slide.

Over the years there has been an ever increasing amount of regulatory and media focus on the behaviour of senior management but, so far, most of the cases that we hear about are where the numbers are huge, the personalities involved are well known or the problem has become so deep rooted that it has taken the company down.

In 2005 L. Dennis Kozlowski, the former chief executive of Tyco, was convicted for using company funds for everything from buying expensive works of art to holding an extravagant (allegedly two million dollar) 'Caligulesque' birthday party for his wife on the Mediterranean island of Sardinia. Then there was Jack Welch's retirement package, which became public as a result of his wife's divorce settlement claim. The sins of the flesh! The retirement package was quickly adjusted to something more reasonable as an apparent reaction to the bad press that it received. There were huge pension payoffs for Percy Barnevik and Goran Lindahl, made by an ABB Group that a couple of years later was nearly out of business because of its debt position. After these pension payments became public, it was agreed that a significant portion would be repaid. There was the CEO who had negotiated a $22 million pay-off if his contract was terminated, for whatever reason. Just imagine - this individual could be fired because of decreasing shareholder value and then, to add insult to injury, take another $22 million out of the shareholders' pockets on his way out of the door. Situations like that defy common sense and you have to ask how they are allowed to happen.

These individuals are, or were, all extremely well compensated by way of salaries, bonuses, share options and all their other perks by their respective employers. They are far from impoverished, so why do they need to go so far over the score? Is it greed, arrogance, ego, the need to maintain a lifestyle or what? The drivers in each case are probably different but the impact on the shareholders is always negative.

Sadly, in the cases of Messrs Barnevik and Welch, we saw much admired and widely respected business leaders having their hard-won reputations tarnished for some (albeit not insignificant) personal gain.

At the heart of all the comments in this book is a conviction that, in return for the income they receive, whether it be a straightforward salary or a salary plus bonus, share options and other add-ons, managers should direct all their best efforts at maximising value for the enterprise, whatever its nature, over the long term and that this should be reflected in all their day-to-day behaviour. Unfortunately, in the typical publicly quoted company, all the drivers and pressure in a manager's day-to-day life seem to be directed at maximising short-term results and all their actions and decisions are focussed accordingly, even though this is rarely in the best long-term interest of the shareholders. Very many management incentive programmes exacerbate this problem, but more about that later.

The logic that managers use to defend short-term decision-making goes along the lines that, 'if I don't meet the short-term targets, I won't be around to worry about the long-term so I'll focus on what matters to me'. The Directors and senior operating managers of most companies will probably go through a strategic planning process, at least once each year, that sets a course and direction for the business for, maybe, the next three or five years. The intent is good but a couple of bad quarterly results will soon divert their attention away from the long-term plans and get them focussed squarely on short-term survival. It's an old saying but it is absolutely true – when you are up to your backside in alligators, it's difficult to remember that you were hired to drain the swamp! Current performance is certainly important (particularly to those who are tasked with delivering it!) but I would argue that it is not in the best interests of the shareholders over the long-term if the achievement of short-term results, by any means possible, becomes the only thing that matters to the managers of their business.

It is interesting that exactly the opposite situation seems to exist in the public sector where the argument that "we take a long-term view" seems to substitute for any kind of serious short-term accountability. The Strategic Plans are there but they will never be achieved because the actions that are needed to get the organisation from here to there will never be identified, much less assigned and made to happen.

How many shareholders really recognise the seriousness and depth of these problems in their businesses or organisations? The answer is 'probably not very many'.

How many companies or organisations can truly claim to be well and efficiently managed at all levels? The answer again is 'probably not very many'.

These issues are explored in more detail in the subsequent chapters but, for the moment, I will give you a summary of what I mean.

In business, the impact on the shareholders happens at both the Profit and Loss Account (P&L) and share value levels.

Items that impact the company's P&L include:

- Money that is spent unnecessarily on things which benefit individual employees, or groups of employees, but which have no added-value for the company.

- Payments made to employees, which are in excess of the value that those employees add to the business.

- Payments made to employees, which are in excess of the market value of those employees.

- The direct costs of losing employees, including costs of hiring replacements, training costs and learning curve costs.

- Sub-optimal performance.

- The loss of market position caused when good employees move to direct competitors.

- Excessive severance costs.

Items that impact share value include:

- Sub-optimal performance.

- Analyst and investor perception of the company and its culture.

- Competitive disadvantage when good employees are lost to direct competitors, adversely affecting relative performance.

In the case of the public sector, the impacts are to the P & L and the ultimate loser is the taxpayer.

The lawsuit by investors against the Walt Disney Corporation served to illustrate how some of the management sins can cost the shareholders at both the P&L Account and share value levels. Here we had arrogance, bullying and profligacy by the bucket-load and, if it had not been so serious, it would have provided the basis for a great cartoon. - Walt Disney's 'Bullies of the Boardroom' has a certain ring to it. The company has moved on from those troubled days but the lessons should not be forgotten.

For shareholders, these problems present challenges at two levels. Firstly` there is the problem of how to recognise that management is not delivering (and is not going to deliver) the best platform for long-term success. The second part is, once the problem has been recognised, to figure out the best thing to do about it. I don't have any neat packaged solutions but will explore some possibilities in my final chapter.

Many managers who read this book will, I am sure, proclaim their innocence and argue that their short-term behaviour is driven directly by the shareholders' demand for current results that will sustain or boost the share price *now*. In response, I would suggest that it is more about the senior management and Board of Directors not wanting to give bad, or even slightly disappointing, news to the shareholders. The day-to-day priorities and pressures within the business come from senior management and *not* from the shareholders and, all too often, the senior managers are driven solely by what's good for the senior management.

To ensure that shareholder value is maximised over the long-term, companies and organisations need major changes to current mind-sets and behavioural characteristics, and the structure of compensation plans has to change so that they actively encourage and promote the delivery of long-term success.

None of this is going to be achieved over night.

Chapter 2: Arrogance

Arrogant: aggressively and offensively self-assertive; having or showing too high an opinion of one's own abilities or importance; impudently over-presumptive.

(Chambers 21st Century Dictionary)

I am deliberately presenting my seven sins in alphabetical order so that the reader doesn't see any ranking of seriousness that is not intended. First up, therefore, is 'A' for 'Arrogance'.

The manager's role, in the vast majority of cases, includes the requirement to lead and motivate other people and it should be obvious that a high level of self-assurance and confidence is essential if this is to be done effectively. Whether you are a manager in business, an officer in the military or the manager of a football team, the people in your business, brigade or team must have faith in your ability, judgement and decisions. If they don't have faith in your ability then you are wasting your time trying to lead them anywhere. You must also have their respect because without the respect of your employees you will find yourself leading a one-man charge. Unfortunately, the line between respect and fear is a very thin one and, as a manager, you need to recognise the difference. People who respect you will both follow you and look out for you. People who follow you through fear (because they are scared not to) will give lip-service to your success and well-being but will constantly be waiting for you to fail and to fall.

If you are managing through fear, don't waste your time looking around for help when the wolves are closing in on you because help won't be there. Your employees will be safely in the branches of nearby trees waiting for the carnage that is about to unfold in front of them.

The potential downside that is always lurking in the confident manager is that, once that confidence becomes arrogance, it can be a huge turn-off for the people who work for and around him.

Arrogance comes in a lot of different forms. In countries like India, Nigeria and Egypt, management arrogance has its roots in social structures such as the caste system, the tribal hierarchy or other social or religious segregations. It can also be based on something as simple as inherited wealth versus poverty, as was prevalent in the UK in our not too distant history. In Germany, France and Italy I see much management arrogance arising as a direct product of the ranking system that is built into the employment laws. I remember a Financial Controller in Italy who reported to me, who insisted that his staff call him 'Signore', or 'Mr', just because he was Dirigente (the official executive class). When I first came across this I thought that he was joking but, sadly, he was quite serious about it. I have also seen examples of similar behaviour in both Germany and France and, occasionally it must be said, in the UK. (Although there is no doubt that UK industry has become much more Americanised in this regard than has the rest of 'fortress Europe'.)

Having said that, it's not so many years ago (late nineteen-eighties) that I worked for a company in England where all the senior managers were referred to as 'Mister', where there was a 'dining-room' for management and a 'canteen' for the rest of the staff and where women were not allowed to attend functions in the Boardroom. It was a structure that was ended when the company was taken over by a more forward-thinking organisation and, needless to say, very few of the 'old school' senior managers survived the transition. I actually attended the first Boardroom dinner at which lady staff members were guests and I must say that I was fully expecting the soup to be poured into their laps, the table to collapse or the ceiling to fall in on us!

The Americans have their own unique form of 'nouvelle' arrogance that has nothing to do with religion, breeding or family wealth. It's not as immediately obvious as good old-fashioned arrogance because it's disguised under the mantle of friendly informality. The US education system instils self-confidence into pupils from an early age, which I think is a great thing. However, it can also have a downside and anyone who has dealt with Americans in business (or even come across a bus-load of noisy American tourists) will be familiar with what can be the result. Most people would describe it as brashness or loudness rather than arrogance but when you scratch below the informality in American management you will find that a goodly proportion of American managers suffer from plain, simple, common or garden arrogance.

So what's wrong with a bit of arrogance?

In truth, it can be a real asset but the important word here is 'bit'. An excess of arrogance is only an asset to the person who carries it. Arrogant people in business will, in many cases, rise to a position above their own level of competence and the result will be sub-par performance from the shareholders' viewpoint and a lot of collateral damage.

As someone once told me, when a manager becomes a legend in his own mind it is time for the organisation to beware!

Arrogance manifests itself in phrases like 'my way or no way', 'when I want your view, I'll ask for it', 'my time is too valuable for this' and 'what the hell do they know about it?' Arrogant people are typically poor listeners who speak across others and wear their short attention span like a badge of achievement. They put others down publicly without thinking about the impact on feelings or, worse still, they put others down publicly to get a cheap laugh at others' expense. We had a President who would let people know that he was bored with what they were saying, or that he had seen enough of their presentation, by imperiously announcing, "Okay that's enough. Thirty days — next case." Another of his well-worn public 'put-downs' was, "Everybody has a role in the organisation, Smith, even if it's only as a bad example to others!"

The first couple of times that you hear these, seemingly off-the-cuff, comments it's difficult to resist a smile but when you are hearing the same catch-phrase for the umpteenth time it can't even claim any amusement value as a saving grace.

Indirectly the public put-down is also a form of bullying and this is a good example of the 'sins' blurring and blending.

There was an ex-boss of mine who liked to publicly taunt his finance staff with a laughing (and over-used), "Bean-counters are like racehorses – you ride them until they're knackered and then you go out and buy yourself another one". Every time I heard that particular 'funny' I had a strong inclination to test the pain threshold of his tender bits with the toe of my shoe. Alas, we accountants need to preserve our professional image (and I needed the job), so I resisted the temptation. One day when the numbers weren't showing the answer he was looking for, he said to me, "Damn it Campbell, can't you get some good bean-counters into this organisation?" I pointed out that the fact that he now recognised that there were good bean-counters and bad bean-counters rather than just the generic group of bean-counters was a sign of real progress. Although I am making a joke of it, the reality is that, however you view it and however it manifests itself, arrogance is not a very attractive characteristic.

Recognising the negative impacts of arrogance in one's own behaviour is not easy. An example that brought this solidly home to me was when one of our senior Project Managers left the Company. I had disagreed with him on a number of occasions and had (deliberately and knowingly) embarrassed him in a couple of different group situations. I had wrongly assumed that he accepted my behaviour as part of the normal give-and-take of day-to-day business life and that there were no hard feelings - after all the man was a seasoned Project

Manager and well able to take care of himself! How wrong I was. In his exit interview, in response to the question of whether he would consider future employment with the Company, the individual wrote, "Not so long as Ian Campbell is the Finance Director". Obviously my arrogant behaviour had had an impact on this individual that I would not have dreamed possible. The truly arrogant would, of course, have dismissed his criticism with a comment like, "I always knew he was over-sensitive" or (worse), "I always had him tagged as a bit of a wimp". Fortunately I was unable to be so dismissive, so maybe there is some hope of salvation for me. I would be lying if I claimed that the experience had cured me but it had definitely taught me a useful lesson.

From the organisational (and therefore the shareholders') perspective, the problem is that when a leader's excessive arrogance starts to drive the shape and calibre of the organisation around him, he will lose the benefit of synergies or contradictory views because many people will simply tell him what he wants to hear rather than to speak their minds and invite grief. When they were asked for their opinion on something important, a catch-phrase amongst some of the managers in one of the companies that I worked for was "I agree with Joe" ('Joe' being our President) and it encapsulated people's reluctance to say anything in public to disagree with the President. It was invariably said with a smile but the underlying sentiment was a serious one.

Joe was smart, charismatic and successful but his arrogance meant that he probably didn't get the best out of the pool of management talent available to him in the business. As a business we did well but perhaps we could have done even better. The arrogant leader will tend to sever relations with the people who strongly challenge his views and, over time, will inevitably become surrounded by 'yes-men'. These 'yes-men' will only serve to enhance the view in his own mind that he is a capable, popular and much-admired boss. It's a classic snowball effect. To express it in the words that I have used before, 'he becomes a legend in his own mind'. The relationship between the leader and the people who work for him will become more artificial and superficial and the missing ingredient is respect. Rather than establishing a strong balanced team in which there are in-built checks and balances, the arrogant leader will eventually build a team around him that nurtures his arrogance.

When I was a young Controller working in Africa, we had a Regional Manager who could have been the caricature used for the cafe owner, Rene, in the TV series 'Allo, allo'. (Obviously he was a Frenchman). Anyway, he made a fairly major decision related to our subsidiary that caused a high level of concern and consternation within our local management team. After a lot of discussion within the team it was decided that the situation was serious enough that we should broach our concerns with him and, like a crusading idiot, I volunteered to be the spokesperson for the team. I put our concerns into a carefully crafted memo, attached it to the proverbial pigeon's leg and sent it on its way. I received no acknowledgement or response. Several months later I was in Switzerland for the annual budget meetings and, when we assembled in the bar for pre-dinner drinks on the first evening, I was asked to step to one side by the Regional Manager. Even after more than forty years I'm sure that I am pretty close to repeating his words verbatim.

"Ah Cam*bell* (no 'p' and emphasis on the 'bell'), I wanted you to know zat I got zis note zat you sent me and I did not appreciate it one leettle bit. When I 'aff made a decision it is not your position to question it and, if zis 'appens again, your career 'ere is feeneshed. Is zis clear?"

I mumbled a quick "yes" (as I tried to put myself out of my misery by drowning in my beer) and then galloped away, with my tail between my legs, towards some more friendly faces.

It wasn't what he said that was the issue for me, it was the way that he said it. From his perspective we (or rather I) had questioned his judgement on an issue that hadn't required our input. However, his message could have been delivered more gently but just as effectively and with a better result than was achieved. I had been unsettled in my work for a while and his speech was pretty much the last straw for me so I found another job and left several months later. I was good at my job and getting bright young Controllers to work in Africa wasn't easy. My skills were marketable and his ill-chosen words caused a lot more pain and cost for the Company than they did for me.

I had been naive (and a tad stupid) but the way the Frenchman had handled this issue over pre-dinner drinks with a relatively inexperienced employee from two tiers down the organisation was a piece of supreme arrogance.

Without his arrogance the situation could have been handled so much better. Perhaps something along the lines of.........

"I received your note and I appreciate the concerns and input of you and your colleagues. However, in this instance, there were factors involved that none of you were privy to and, of course, the decision was only reached after serious consideration within my own management team. I am sure that, despite your concerns, I can count on you all to support the decision that I have made"..............

I would still have been suitably chastened but would have appreciated the time he had taken to explain the situation to me and would almost certainly have stayed with the company for some time longer than I did.

A friend of mine worked for an aggressively acquisitive listed US Company, which went through several years of doing expensive deals and then struggling with the integration of its acquired businesses. The company's aggressively acquisitive nature made it attractive to investors but its trading results were inconsistent and generally disappointing. At a meeting with a group of his senior managers, the CEO told his audience, with absolute confidence and conviction, that the company's share price would be eighty dollars within a few years. (It was then somewhere between thirty-five and forty dollars). He went on to tell them that he had competent people working for him who ran the business and that his personal 'raison d'etre' was to manage the investors and the analysts. He also told them that it was something that he was very good at! It was a case of "you run the business and I'll manage the investors and the analysts and we will all get rich". That speech probably rated an eight-out-of-ten on the arrogance scale. For a short time the company's share price moved positively and senior managers boosted their bank accounts via some short term stock option schemes. Acquisitions served to hide underlying business weaknesses and flaws for a while but it wasn't going to last. In the ensuing years the company's shares consistently under-performed their industry peers but, despite that, the CEO stayed in power for many years before he was eventually ousted. The market value of the shares was distorted by a couple of stock splits but the eighty dollars was never achieved and now the value is in single figures.

What this CEO seemed to overlook is that, if you run a successful business, which consistently delivers on (or close to) its commitments, you don't need to put a lot of effort or expertise into managing (or 'spinning'?) the investors and the analysts. No amount of arrogance, charm or spin can ever substitute for real performance in the long term.

Back in the mid-nineteen-eighties two major US Corporations were in advanced negotiations over the potential sale of a major division of one of them to the other. The potential acquirer was a head-to-head competitor of the division being sold and the inevitable rationalisation that would follow acquisition meant that the fate of several thousand jobs was hanging in the balance. The story goes, that most of the legwork, due diligence and other formalities had been completed and they were trying to schedule a meeting of the two CEOs to get a 'handshake' on a deal. The CEO of the selling company allegedly told his people, "I am a busy person and, if they are serious about buying, their CEO will need to get on a plane and come here."

. You know what's coming next, don't you?

The CEO of the buying company allegedly told his people, "I am a busy person and, if they want our money, their CEO will need to get on a plane and come here."

The two CEOs did not meet and the deal did not happen. I cannot swear that this story is true but I worked for the division that was being sold and the story came from a very knowledgeable source within the senior management. It is certainly credible. If it *is* true, I would suggest that if those two self-important men had been kids (instead of just behaving like kids), their Dads would have smacked their heads together and told them to grow up.

As a continuation of the same story, it's interesting to note that the CEO of the selling company had been hired by the Corporation a couple of years earlier to shake things up and breathe new life into a staid, conservative and risk averse environment. Early in his tenure he went on a road show, preaching to the employees about how he was going to increase shareholder value. (The shares had been trading in a narrow range of twenty to twenty-five dollars for quite some time). He and his entourage arrived at each of the company's major facilities in a fleet of limousines, complete with his own personal security team. He took off his jacket, loosened his tie, rolled-up his sleeves and told the assembled managers and supervisors that they could call him 'Harry'. He extolled them to great deeds. The red ink bottles could all be thrown away as every business in the group was "going to be in the black all the way" from that day forward and the group's share price was going to surge upwards.

Five or six years later the share price was still in the mid-twenties before an unsolicited 'slam-dunk' cash bid for the company (around forty dollars per share if I remember rightly) gave the shareholders some reward for their patience. Amazingly, despite the years that this company had suffered in the doldrums under his captaincy, 'Harry' rode on to bigger and better things with his reputation as a crusading agent of change still largely intact. He was certainly over-endowed with confidence and he could certainly talk a good fight.

Arrogance can also lead to bad deals. How many times have the Directors of a company pursuing an acquisition allowed the price to be pushed beyond anything that made commercial sense because their egos wouldn't let them pull out of the deal? Far too often I would suggest. Royal Bank of Scotland's take-over of ABN-Ambro was driven through by the key players at RBS apparently regardless of the commercial realities and that was a real stinker. The Venture Capitalists are a good exemplar in this regard. Yes they are greedy but, in the words of Kenny Roger's song, they know when to hold, know when to fold up, know when to walk away and know when to run!

Another manifestation of arrogance is the 'one-time' (or even 'no-time') expert. How many managers do you know who can speak, apparently knowledgeably, on pretty much any subject at the drop of a hat? Quite a few, I suspect.

The one-time expert is a person who sees something once and instantly (and miraculously) knows all about it. The no-time expert is even more gifted because he doesn't even need to see the subject. The mere mention of it in his presence is enough to endow him with a detailed knowledge that most of us mortals would take weeks, months or years to acquire. The fact is that very many of these instant experts speak a high percentage of bullshit, but they do it with such conviction that they are rarely challenged or taken to task. When their views are taken by others as credible input to the decision-making process, they can do real damage. It's sad to say, but many successful careers have been built on this ability and the upward progression of these individuals does absolutely nothing positive for shareholder value.

I had a peer on one senior management team who had a view on any and every subject even though the subject was one that he knew nothing about. He would say something completely bizarre or naive, with absolute sincerity and certainty, but was rarely challenged. I must confess that I never figured out whether this was because everybody knew him for what he was and let him talk without taking on board what he said, or whether it was because everyone else around the table was too embarrassed to confess that they didn't understand what he was talking about! It was probably a mix of the two. Apparently he was an excellent and innovative

Engineer and I will address the issue of functional expertise versus management ability in Chapter 6.

There have been many studies that have demonstrated the benefits that can be gained through synergistic interaction and many more studies that have shown the benefits that can accrue from having teams comprised of members who offer a variety of different styles and characteristics (balanced teams). Where arrogance leads to autocracy, all these benefits are lost.

The sting in the tail is that success is a breeding ground for arrogance. When that happens, it is extremely difficult to recognise that an erstwhile successful manager has crossed the threshold into excessive arrogance and moved into a phase where he is likely to create future under-performance.

Evaluating, in financial terms, the negative effects of excessive management arrogance on the shareholders is impossible. That there *is* an effect, that it is negative and that it is probably significant are incontrovertible.

Chapter 3: Bullying

Bully: a person who hurts, frightens or torments weaker or smaller people.

Bullying: to act like a bully towards someone; to threaten or persecute them; to force them to do something they do not want to do.

(Chambers 21st Century Dictionary)

If I had a Pound, a Dollar, or a Euro, for every time that I had heard someone being told "If you do that again, I'll fire your arse" or "If you can't handle it, we'll get somebody who can" or "You need to be careful because you're pissing off some important people around here", I would be a rich man. Threats, intimidation and even persecution are rife in the workplace, most particularly in American companies and companies that adopt an American style of management.

An ex-boss of mine explained the philosophy rather well. He said, "In our company we use a carrot-and-stick approach to motivation. First we place a large carrot in the employee's backside and then we use the stick to hammer it in." It was said in a joking way but the reality of the Company's management style wasn't so far divorced from his joke.

I remember going to another boss of mine in the same company with what I felt were some serious concerns about my role, responsibilities and career path at the time. He listened, with obvious impatience to what I had to say and then said, "Yep, shit happens!" That was it – conversation over. There are no marks for recognising that I was working for an employee-focussed and caring organization!

At the same company, in a management discussion about the potential for Union representation being heisted on us at one of our UK manufacturing sites, our HR Manager was explaining how, if the majority of the workforce wanted representation, it would be difficult for the company to stop it happening. The President of the company abruptly told him that, in the President's view, it was the HR Manager's job to keep the Union out and if the Union came in his job would no longer be needed. Not precisely "If you can't handle it, we'll get somebody who can", but pretty damned close! This took place in front of a number of other managers (including me) - a classic public put down.

Every manager wants to hear how things can, and will, be done and no manager wants to hear excuses or reasons why things cannot be made to happen. I used to hate it when my managers told me why something couldn't be done and offered me no potential compromises or alternatives. However, understanding the facts and the risks in any situation is an essential first step towards successful action. A boss who refuses to hear bad news, or who doesn't have time to hear about one of his manager's difficulties with a particular issue that is important for the business, is already high on the arrogance scale. It is a very short jump from arrogance to bullying and I have seen lots of managers crossing that divide, including myself at times.

In countries that offer some security of employment under their laws, bullying is less effective as a management tool. On the other hand, where it is relatively easy for employers to get rid of staff, bullying can be an effective way of getting compliance and it is widely used. In the UK it is still relatively easy for a ruthless company to get rid of employees although there may be a significant cost involved. 'Compromise Agreements' that offer the employee the opportunity to put a chunk of cash in their pocket and go away quietly are becoming more and more widely used.

The threat of termination of employment is the ultimate sanction and is probably the single most widely used form of bullying. America is the prime example among countries where this happens, although recent years have seen some mitigation there because of the anti-discrimination laws. It has certainly become harder to use bullying as a management tool in the US when dealing with women or ethnic minorities because of the risk of the company ending up embroiled in a discrimination suit. However, the white male below forty years of age is still a largely unprotected species in the US and is fair game for the bully. Based on my own experience, I can't think of another country that comes anywhere close to America in terms of its bullying management style. Bullying undoubtedly thrives elsewhere but the simple threat of firing doesn't have the same impact where the labour laws and formalised disciplinary and grievance procedures offer protection to the employee. In these situations the bullying necessarily becomes a bit more subtle and less overt.

Even in the countries that offer some protection under their laws, it is important to recognise that the threat of dismissal is something that can cause considerable distress and concern to the individual employee who is being threatened as well as to friends and relatives who are close to him. To try to work in a motivated and effective way when you feel the Sword of Damocles hanging over your head must be impossible, even for the most robust of characters. Managers will say, "I was only joking", but very few employees who are threatened with dismissal see it as a joke. As a manager, you will find that it is frequently necessary to encourage, cajole and push people to meet deadlines and targets and it is essential, for the good of the whole organisation, that you keep concerted pressure on under-performing staff. What you have to guard against is stepping over the line that divides reasonable pressure from bullying. The consequences of bullying can never, in the long term, be positive and bullying should have no place in a well-managed workplace.

Unfortunately, what constitutes bullying is not well defined and it is often in the eye of the beholder. One person's version of encouragement, cajoling or reasonable pressure is another person's idea of bullying.

I had a Financial Controller reporting to me who, in my view, was struggling to stay on top of his job and who compounded the situation by failing to carry out any sort of reasonableness review on his own work product or that of his staff before it was issued. He had a deserved and unenviable reputation of presenting numbers to senior management that contained naive and obvious arithmetic mistakes. This culminated in a very frustrated CEO coming out from an operational review and telling me never to let this individual present any numbers to his Senior Management Team again, unless I had personally checked them before they were presented.

The individual concerned was the Controller of an eighty million pound business. He was both well qualified for the job that he was doing and well remunerated for doing it. There was no training gap, he wasn't new to the role and I felt that the Company was entitled to expect a higher level of performance from him than it was getting. I certainly wasn't going to start checking the arithmetic accuracy of his work! Overall the individual's performance was below expectations but it was marginal rather than disastrous so there were no clear-cut grounds for termination. Also, within some members of our Senior Management Team, there was still a belief that the individual had it within himself to get on top of his job and, in particular, to resolve the issue of carelessness. In classic fashion, his formal Performance Appraisals had ranged from adequate to good and it was only the most recent one (done by me) that focussed on some of his weaknesses in the hope that he would start to address them. In order to try and resolve this unsatisfactory situation, in one way or the other, I formalised some short-term objectives for the individual to try to help him get on top of the whole scope of the job and I started to monitor his performance against these objectives on a rolling basis. I also started to formally document some of his more obvious cock-ups. Both actions were designed to help him, but also to provide the foundations for a properly constructed disciplinary case *if* he failed to improve his performance. On the positive side, he was being given a chance but, on the negative side, he was under serious pressure to perform and he knew it. Word soon reached me that his CV was on the street and that he was very actively looking for another job. As it transpired, it took quite a long time but eventually he found another job and moved on.

That individual's heartfelt interpretation of the pressure that he was put under by me was that he was being bullied.

Even with the advantage of hindsight, I don't think he was, but mine is obviously a heavily biased view and I'll leave it to you, the reader, to form your own opinion. However, it does serve as an excellent illustration of how differently the same situation can appear when viewed from opposite sides. As a friend of mine used to tell me, "It's the same game watched by two different spectators standing on opposite sides of the pitch."

"But how does a bullying management style affect the shareholders and potentially impair shareholder value?" I hear you ask.

Resilient and independent people may accept that a bullying culture exists at their workplace and learn to co-exist with it. On the other hand, they might decide that it's not an environment that they want to work in, and leave because of it. The loss of *any* employee has a real cost to the business (and therefore to the shareholders) at the very minimum in simple terms of recruiting and training a replacement. The loss of a high-potential employee has an additional impact through the loss of the future value-adding activities of that employee. In some cases there may be the 'double whammy' of seeing those value-adding activities move across the street to a direct competitor.

Managers and shareholders should be under no illusions – a lot of good employees will simply not put up with a bullying culture and will move on. Less resilient and less independent people will either join the culture and become bullies themselves or become victims of it. Victims of bullying are likely to have more time away from work due to sickness, and the incidence of stress related cases in the business is likely to go up. Even when they are at work, employees who feel threatened and intimidated are not motivated, are not effective and don't give the shareholders fair value for the cost of their employment.

More damagingly, employees who are seriously concerned about their job can do some very irrational things. The management of one company that I dealt with had come under intense pressure for more profit on a month-by-month basis from their Product Group Management. (This was a small specialist manufacturing company that was part of a major division of a global group). Unable to deliver the required results, and faced with monthly 'beat up' sessions, they started to get creative with their numbers. It was a simple case of 'credit P&L and debit the Balance Sheet' – showing profits that had never been earned. They delivered the demanded profit but their inventory figure started going steadily upwards and they had some really questionable amounts in the areas of accounts receivable and prepayments. Revenues were being recognised on an increasingly cavalier basis (much earlier than was proper) and related costs were being left on the Balance Sheet. An example is when a five-year Licence Agreement was signed with a sister company in India, under which the Indian Company was to pay a fixed annual fee in return for the granting of a licence to build certain of the Company's products. The Agreement also required the Company to provide the Indian Company with all necessary and related on-going engineering support. The ink was no sooner dry on the Agreement than the total of the five-year's fees was recorded as income. There was absolutely nothing in the structure of the Agreement to support taking the income on anything other than a year-by-year basis and the decision to book it all to income up-front was driven purely by the pressure being put on the management for results.

After three or four years of these shell games, this £25 million turnover business had a staggering £7 million 'black hole' in its Balance Sheet. Inventory, accounts receivable and prepayments were all overstated, with the major problem being in inventory. When their Product Group Management discovered the problem, they decided that it was too big to digest in one mouthful and set about amortising the non-existent assets over four or five years. It was amazing that they were able to blow smoke up the external auditors' backsides for as long as they did, but the combination of a shaky cost system, an innovative Controller and 'materiality' in the context of the worldwide group results meant that this situation remained undiscovered for way too long. With an inherently unprofitable business now burdened with writing-off the fictitious assets, the results worsened, the problem could no longer be hidden at the Product Group level and management changes were made.

Amazingly, the arch-bully survived, presumably to continue his antics elsewhere in his Division. The management of the mother company obviously thought that his industry-knowledge and ability to deliver results (?) outweighed the collateral damage caused to some of the people who worked for him. A bit like a General who wins battles but is profligate with the lives of his troops!

Of course bullying can take less obvious forms, including more carefully veiled threats and blackmail. I had a colleague who was living and working in a very pleasant location in the Far East when the company decided that it wanted to move him to a similar level of position in the North of England. Being from the North East of Scotland my colleague felt that anything in England was just as much of an overseas posting as the Far East but without the benefit of the standard of living afforded by an expatriate assignment. Somewhat less importantly, it lacked the opportunity to accumulate some serious Air Miles and he and his family had been enjoying the year-round hot weather. The way he saw it, the job wasn't in his home base, it wasn't a promotion and it was negative from a lifestyle perspective. After due consideration, he politely declined. A couple of different people (including myself) tried very hard to persuade him to the contrary but without success. Eventually he got a call from the company's Chief Financial Officer (CFO) and, when it became clear that my colleague wasn't going to change his mind, the CFO played his ace.

The gist of what he said went like this:

"Of course there are likely to be some broader organisational changes coming up and, if you don't accept this assignment, I cannot guarantee how long there will be a job for you in the Far East. Unfortunately there may not be anything anywhere else for you if this role is filled in the meantime. I do not want to put pressure on you but I suggest that you think very carefully about the consequences of your refusal."

My colleague had the sense to bite his tongue and promise to give the matter some more thought but he was upset, disappointed and offended by the not very subtle threat. After several more-balanced conversations with (and a lot of persuasion from) other people, my colleague eventually agreed to make the move. However, I would assume that the bullying CFO believes, to this day, that it was his intervention and persuasive skills that did the trick!

I can only recall one instance of physical (rather than mental) bullying by a manager in the workplace. The culprit was a manufacturing manager who had a quick temper and a reputation for breaking or throwing things. He was a big, raw, loose-limbed American and tales of some of his exploits had preceded his arrival in the U.K. I'll call him 'Bill' for present purposes. My favourite story was that Bill had been looking for some engineering drawings and had eventually found out that they were locked in the desk of one of his supervisors who had gone away on holiday. Bill took a fire-axe to the desk. After retrieving the drawings, he proceeded to trash the desk and then told anyone that was within hearing range that, "This desk had better not be touched until that ******* has got back from his vacation. I want it here as a warning to all of you!"

On another occasion, Bill apparently hurled a hard-hat across the meeting-table at someone who had upset him. Fortunately, either his aim was bad or he aimed to miss because no serious damage was done.

I vividly remember Bill arriving at my office door one morning. Filling up most of the doorframe, he announced in his most menacing tone, "Campbell, you are pissing me off." There was no, "good morning", no further explanation and he was obviously upset. I didn't have a clue what he was referring to and, given that he was filling up the only doorway and the window was closed, I didn't have a suitable route for a sharp exit. Instead, I fixed him with a stare and said, "That's good. I'm glad that I'm doing something right. The only pity is that it probably wasn't deliberate." For a moment I thought he was going to explode but then he visibly relaxed, expressed some serious doubts about the marital status of my parents and then laughed. Like most bullies, he was fine if you took him on and backed him up but a lot of people were unreasonably intimidated by his pugnacious, physically threatening style.

The one environment in which I have seen a bullying style being effective in driving a business forward in a positive way is during the formative years of a small business that is led by an entrepreneurial owner. In this situation, the person who is carrying all the risk is certainly entitled to adopt a "do what I say or get out" approach, and a directive and pushy decision-maker is probably what the business needs. However, this asset becomes a liability as the business starts to grow, because the typical bullying owner doesn't accept advice easily and will usually have trouble and keeping strong, good quality managers in the business. I have come across many examples of this over the years and very many of these fast growing, entrepreneur led, family style businesses reach a point in their evolution where they start to under-perform as a direct result of the owner-manager's abrasive style and dogged determination to do things his own way.

I was instrumental in securing some senior, part-time financial assistance for one of our owner-led suppliers who was having some difficulties with his Bank Manager but the arrangement fell apart after a very short period. To help with the company's cash flow, the interim accountant suggested that the owner and his immediate family should curtail some of their more excessive, company-supported expenses. Changing the Aston Martin and the Range Rover for less exotic carriages, at least until the cash situation was normalised, would be a good start! That suggestion went down like the proverbial lead-balloon and he and the company parted ways shortly thereafter. I should add that this particular accountant had been deliberately selected for this role because he had worked successfully for many years in an entrepreneur owner led business so he understood the risks and the pitfalls of that environment and knew how to handle them. Despite all his experience and skills he had walked head-on into the immovable wall of somebody who simply is not prepared to listen to advice or reason.

Where people work together (be it in an office, factory, shop, film studio or whatever) there will always be sexual banter, sexual liaisons and even genuine love. No amount of rules, regulations or laws will stop it. However, from the employer's perspective, the difficulties lie in finding the boundary between welcome attentions and unwelcome attentions and in trying to prevent undesirable or threatening situations from developing. A lovers' tiff, between what were previously consenting adult employees in a happy relationship, can suddenly be twisted into a sexual harassment suit involving the company.

Genuine sexual harassment in the workplace is in fact just another form of bullying. Employees go over the boundaries of acceptable behaviour either in the arrogant belief that the target of their harassment will be flattered by their attentions or with the belief of the bully that their victim will be too timid or too frightened to complain.

Sexual harassment is certainly not the sole province of men but we do tend to have an affinity for it. I remember a female manager complaining to me that our Vice President of Human Resources (of all people) was a 'chauvinist sleaze-bag' who, on being introduced to an attractive woman, would visually inspect her from the ankles up to the face and then back down again. I am sure you lady readers will have all met at least one senior manager like that. Anyway, another female employee who was party to the conversation told us that, when it had happened to her, she had deliberately fixed her gaze on the offending man's crotch as she spoke to him. In her words, "he couldn't get out of the room quick enough and never tried that stunt on me again".

In a very similar vein, I was talking to one of the secretaries one day and my boss's name came up in the conversation. She chuckled and said, "Oh yes, he's spoken to me a few times. He's the one who always talks to my boobs rather than to my face!"

There is no doubt that shareholders need managers in their business who can push and cajole additional performance out of others but it has to be done in a positive and motivating way. For many years I worked in, and was an integral part of, a bullying management culture that was second to very few. It was a challenging, never boring, often wearing, testosterone-driven environment. I thrived on it but I still have the sense to realise that when the bullies are running the company it is inevitably going to cost the shareholders lots of money and cause them lots of problems. There will be no lack of decisions and no lack of action but short-term thinking will rule and lots of the things that get done will be sub-optimal or on the boundaries of what is proper. Don't be fooled by the apparent successes because, in the longer term, there will be a heavy price to be paid.

Chapter 4: Greed

Greed: selfish desire in general, e.g. for money.

Greedy: anxious or intensely keen to achieve or get (power, praise, etc).

(Chambers 21st Century Dictionary)

The greed I am concerned with for the purposes of this book is the greed that causes managers to manipulate situations to their own personal pecuniary advantage.

However, it is sins that are the subject of my book rather than crimes, so I will not waste a lot of words delving into situations where the boundary to fraud or theft was crossed. This is, of course, a boundary that can be quite indistinct (particularly in areas like employee expense claims), so I will try to provide some definition.

Employees, including managers, who claim 'reimbursement' on their expenses for items that that they have not expended, or who claim amounts that they are not entitled to, or who represent something to be something that it isn't, are all guilty of theft or fraud in my view. Examples would be tips and taxi fares that are claimed but which were never actually incurred and mileage claims for journeys that weren't actually made. Another old favourite, in the same vein, is the 'piss-up' (or other social gathering) for employees that gets labelled as 'entertainment' and supported by a list of customers' names, none of whom was anywhere near the party.

I have an amusing story here, involving an employee who tried to cross the boundary to fraud in the most incredibly naive way. Apparently, he had scrutinised the Expense Reporting Manual in minute detail to see what he was 'entitled to'. This was a long-term employee who had submitted expense claims without any major problems over a number of years but who, it seems, suddenly decided to get creative. In the sections of the manual covering 'Meals' and 'Entertainment' he noted that tips would be reimbursed up to a maximum of ten per cent of a meal cost. His next expense report wound up on my desk because he had claimed an additional ten per cent for 'tips' on every single line item of his expenses, including the hotel room, phone calls, and laundry! When I say ten per cent, I mean ten per cent. A meal costing £32.34 carried a tip of £3.23 and a laundry bill of £23.27 carried a tip of £2.33. My immediate reaction was that it was a joke but I was assured by the staff in my Finance Department that they had discussed it with the individual concerned and that he was adamant that this was his entitlement per 'Mr Campbell's Expense Manual'.

I decided that enough was enough and that the employee and I needed to have a little private chat.

When I discussed it with him, he was (as I had been warned) adamant that he had done nothing wrong. I pointed out to him that 'reimburse' meant that he had to have actually paid out the amounts before he claimed them back and asked him to confirm that this was indeed his situation.

His answer was, "Your manual says that a ten per cent tip is allowed."

"But did you actually pay out these amounts?" I asked him.

"Your manual says that a ten per cent tip is all right," was the answer.

I tried to make the question even clearer. "Never mind about the manual for the moment, just answer my question. Did you actually pay all the amounts out of your own pocket that you are now claiming back?"

His answer once again was, "Your manual says that a ten per cent tip is all right."

As you can imagine, we didn't get too far on that point because, by then, there was a lot of atmospheric interruption to the communication link between my desk here on earth and the planet Zog where this particular individual seemed to be dwelling. Eventually, because we were making absolutely zero progress towards any logical discussion, I told him to go away and delete all the tips other than those that he had actually paid out. After he had left my office, I banged my head on the desk and punched the wall and found the pain to be soothingly therapeutic. The employee didn't quite do as I had asked but he got quite close. His amended expense report only included tips on meals but it was on every meal and it was still a precisely calculated ten per cent.

Amazingly, there were no subsequent problems with this individual's expenses but the story of the tips went straight into the Finance Department's 'Book of Legends and Records'. The balance of the day's play was recorded for posterity as 'Planet Zog, 3 v Ian Campbell, 0'.

Typically the scope for assuaging individual greed via expense claims is very limited because the rules in this area are usually quite well defined and when you break the rules you have automatically stepped over the line to theft or fraud.

Another story worth telling is that of the Corporate Attorney (of all people) and the fuel bills for his company car. This individual owned a speedboat and would often drive his company car out to the lake at the weekend with the speedboat in tow. One day, the young lady who handled employee expenses asked me if there were many cars that had a petrol tank with a capacity of over forty gallons. She had been reviewing the petrol card billings and noticed that our legal-eagle regularly 'filled up' with forty or forty-five gallons of petrol at a time. A further review showed that this was invariably on a Friday or Saturday and always at the same filling station near the lake. We checked and found that his company car actually had a tank capacity of twenty gallons.

We added up the cost of everything over eighteen gallons per fill during the previous couple of years and presented the young Perry Mason with an invoice for what we reckoned was the minimum cost of his boat fuel.

After a lot of muttering, moaning and protest from his side and some persistent follow-up from our side, he reluctantly agreed to settle the invoice. The sting in the tail was that he paid by cheque and the cheque bounced, which happened to be a felony under local State law. His replacement cheque must have come from a different chequebook, with less rubber in it, and the issue was closed.

All this from our Corporate Attorney, which goes to show that, despite what anyone may say to the contrary, lawyers really are human.

The one area where I believe that it is easy for many managers to feed their personal greed without stepping over the line to the crimes of theft or fraud, is that of incentive bonuses. Incentive programmes inevitably influence employee priorities and behaviour. Indeed, many are designed to do just that. The programmes that altruistically reward employees for overall good performance are few and far between and most programmes are designed to reward employees for delivering specific targets or for moving in a specific direction. It is inevitable that some, many or all of the employees will focus their attention and efforts on the areas that will put additional money in their pocket.

Many, many companies now operate performance and/or results-based management incentive schemes. These are no longer the exclusive province of large companies and such schemes are no longer restricted to the top couple of tiers of management. If you look through the job advertisements in the Times, Telegraph or Financial Times you will see that, nowadays, bonuses are an integral part of the package for many middle, as well as senior, management jobs. Logically, the reason for having these schemes is to incentivise management to work harder and to be more innovative in finding ways of improving business results, thereby increasing shareholder value. However, there is an argument that I have heard on a regular basis, particularly in the US, that says that if the bonus is part of the remuneration package, then it's as good as an entitlement. I absolutely disagree with this view and would counter that, if this is indeed the case, the bonus should be incorporated into the base salary or the salary increase process. Bonuses, if they are to be effective, need to be seen as something extra that reflects and rewards unusual levels of contribution and performance.

If results-based incentive schemes are to work effectively for the shareholders, they must, must, *must* be based on stretch goals and must, must, *must* be structured so they cannot be exploited or abused. Given that smart people can be quite innovative, particularly when it comes to their own well-being, the latter is difficult to achieve.

Most managers are well paid for the job that they do and should, in return, be expected to deliver a high level of personal performance and good business results for the shareholders. If a financial carrot is to be offered for delivering incremental results then these should be incremental to a base that is already pitched at a reasonable level of expectation. If this is not the case, then the shareholders are paying over the odds for the management of their company.

In order to illustrate what I mean, you only need to look at how the management bonus programme works in many companies.

Firstly the criteria, or some combination thereof, are agreed.

Typically the bonus will be based on items such as Cash generation; Income Before Tax [IBT]; Earnings Before Interest, Tax, Depreciation and Amortisation [EBITDA]; Order Intake; Revenues; Receivables Levels; Inventory Levels, On-time Deliveries, Market Share or Share Price. The list is extensive and the key performance measures that are chosen are likely to be tailored to the specific perceived needs of the business at the time the criteria are set. Once the basic criteria have been agreed, then a set of targets is put in place and an incentive plan is designed so that achievement of the targets pays out a certain percentage of the maximum bonus available. The maximum bonus will typically be paid at a specified level of over-performance (exceeding or beating the targets) and there will typically be an entry level somewhere below the targets. The maximum, or 'ceiling', is put in place to protect the company from a situation where unforeseen circumstances or windfall events can give rise to unacceptably high levels of bonus payments.

I once saw a situation where my employers put in place a bonus programme for the sales-force, to try to move some specific very-slow-moving valve inventory. It was anticipated that, even with an incentive in place, selling the valves would be difficult and that orders would typically be for small quantities, coming from across a wide geographical area. It was a plan that had been evolved by our Sales Management. The problem was that they didn't really work through the whole range of 'what ifs' and the necessity for some kind of ceiling was therefore never considered. Soon after the introduction of the bonus programme, our biggest customer in the Middle East issued an enquiry for a large number of valves with a broadly similar specification to our 'obsolete' units. That customer pretty much took the whole of our world-wide inventory of the valves and our salesman in Saudi Arabia thought that all his birthdays had arrived on the same day. His bonus was huge in relation to both his (and everybody else's) normal earnings as well as to the amount of effort that he had put into this particular transaction. The valves moved, one person made out like a bandit and the rest of the sales-force was, to say the least, extremely disgruntled.

A ceiling would have prevented this kind of excessive payment, although it must be recognised that imposing a ceiling has its own drawbacks. With a ceiling in place, management has no incentive to turn in results that exceed the point at which the maximum bonus is paid. Smart management will therefore try to ensure that any excess (be it earnings, cash, stock options or whatever) is carried into the following year with the aid of some appropriate financial engineering or finagling.

A very simple example of a bonus programme structure that illustrates this would be as follows....

Target Cash Generation - £20 million

Bonus range – Zero to 20% of base salary (linear)

Entry level - £12 million Cash Generation

Maximum paid at - £32 million Cash Generation

Because the bonus is calculated on a linear basis, Cash Gen of £15 million would get a 3% bonus, Cash Gen of £20 million (target) would get an 8% bonus and Cash Gen of £30 million would get an 18% bonus. For £32 million (or more) of cash, the maximum bonus of 20% would be paid. This inevitably means that if it looks as if the cash is going to reach [say] £34 million, the management will be looking for ways of using £2 million in the last few days of the year to effectively push £2 million of cash generation to the following year. Pulling forward a cheque run to suppliers generally or making some selective early payments to suppliers are the most obvious and easiest ways of achieving this.

Remember that the logic behind this kind of bonus scheme is that it is supposed to encourage managers to deliver a higher level of performance than they otherwise would, thereby benefiting the shareholders as well as increasing the managers' earning potential.

So, do bonus programmes generally deliver the results that they were intended to deliver?

In my view the answer is a resounding 'No' and I'll explain why.

It's a story of the good, the mediocre and the bad. My father used to tell me that you should always be prepared to put a little more into life than you expect to get out of it. Managers who share that attitude, and are motivated in their work, will give more than one hundred percent effort without the need to dangle additional incentives in front of their noses. These are the 'good'. Other managers are ambivalent and will give a steady seventy or eighty per cent effort regardless of how much they are bribed, cajoled or pushed. These are the 'worker bees' or 'steady-Eddies'. The third category consists of the greedy ones, who will do whatever they can to maximise their personal 'take' out of the business. These are the 'bad', and they are the ones who will work the incentive scheme for their own advantage.

In my view, Jim Collins summed it up very accurately and very succinctly when he wrote, "The right people will do the right things and deliver the best results they're capable of, regardless of the incentive system." No matter what arguments you hear to the contrary, this is an absolute truth. Collins also wrote that "...people are not your most important asset. The *right* people are" and "Letting the wrong people hang around is unfair to all the right people." To think you might actually attain a workforce population of one-hundred-percent 'right' people is a piece of Utopian wishful-thinking, but that shouldn't stop you from striving in that direction.

Increasingly, 'bonus management' is becoming a skill in its own right and the first step in the 'bonus management' process for the potential recipient is to negotiate targets that are as low as possible. Typically, this is a slow and laborious process. Explaining how the current year's good results are an aberration due to a number of favourable non-recurring events and how next year is going to see harder competition with margins being squeezed, has become a management science in some companies. As a result, the amount of management time being spent on this process in some large companies is absolutely criminal. Senior managers in large multi-tiered companies were always caught in the squeeze of trying to balance bullish, global, 'tops down' targets coming from the Board with the sum of bearish 'bottoms up' budgets turned in by their operating companies or divisions. The wider use of results-based management incentive programmes has certainly exacerbated this problem.

There is no benefit to the shareholders in having the business measured against targets that are relatively easy to achieve. There is also a real cost to the shareholders in terms of the management time and effort that is invested in the internally focussed negotiation process and in the big management bonuses that are then, in many cases, paid out to reward nothing better than mediocre performance.

I recall Percy Barnevik, the former CEO of ABB, being quoted as saying that he preferred to have managers who set 'stretch' targets and come close to achieving them rather than managers who set easy targets and exceed them. This is a sentiment that I agree wholeheartedly with, but I have yet to see a management incentive scheme that doesn't promote precisely the opposite behaviour.

In one of my jobs, we would typically know the details of our management incentive programme within the first couple of months of our fiscal year. However there was an occasion when the negotiation and approval process dragged on into the second half of the year. In previous years, the programme had been based on a combination of Cash and P&L performance, with the relative weightings changing from year-to-year. The talk in this particular year was that new orders (referred to as 'bookings' in some businesses) were to be added into the programme, but the relative weightings of the three criteria had not been agreed. At that point, the group as a whole had a major cash problem with substantial long-term debt maturing and a credit rating that had fallen significantly. Around the end of the third quarter, it was announced that the management incentive programme would be based entirely on cash generation. Targets were issued and, for three months, the whole organisation was focussed on little other than generating cash. The Field Sales Force became dedicated receivables chasers, deals were done and the last drop of blood was wrung out of the vendors. Detailed weekly performance reports went upwards and minutely detailed action lists were passed downwards. Verbal beatings were handed down for any shortage against the weekly targets and the members of the finance team who were normally involved in the cash management process were buried in producing reports and explaining the variances. We submitted our week-by-week forecasts to our Head Office and, if the CEO and CFO didn't like the total at the end, they would come back with their own arbitrary and higher target. Explaining variances against an arbitrary target is (as any of you who have tried it will know) a completely meaningless exercise. Nonetheless, being good employees, we diligently made up some plausible sounding answers because it was demanded that we do so. In the final couple of months of the year I was not allowed to pay a single vendor invoice without specific prior approval from the US parent company's CFO and CEO. Believe it or not, I was the Finance Director of a nine-figure turnover business and I needed to get approval from across the Atlantic to pay a fifty-dollar invoice. It was that serious.

During the same period, some innovative person in the US issued an edict that no payroll taxes (PAYE/NI) or VAT payments were to be made in November or December. It was only after a lengthy and bruising process of convincing them that they were instructing us to defy the law that this particular aberration was withdrawn. It was amazing how the organisation could make you feel like the bad guy in this situation when all you were trying to do was to save it from itself!

When we were told that the seriousness of the overall group debt situation required that we exceed all our original targets, our senior management took the opportunity to negotiate an additional 'super bonus' for any over-performance, effectively lifting the previously-set ceiling. With all the effort that was put in and the deals that were done, we handsomely exceeded our original cash generation target and we all enjoyed excellent bonus payments. I accepted mine with good grace but was left with a hollow feeling about how it had been achieved. On a positive note we had helped the wider group to manage its way through a difficult short-term crisis but we had also quite ruthlessly managed and exploited the situation to line our pockets.

However (and it's a giant 'however'), you only get cash once. The first quarter of the next fiscal year was an unmitigated, and totally predictable, disaster for cash. Lots of deals had been done to pull cash forward and, over the six-month period (Quarter 4 of one year and Quarter 1 of the next), the cash performance was probably not much better than it would have been without the crisis behaviour in that fourth quarter. Much was made of just how precarious the group's borrowing position had become but I can't believe that the lending institutions and investors were so naive that they didn't realise that a sudden (almost miraculous) change to a hugely positive cash situation in one calendar quarter would be likely to reverse itself in the subsequent quarter. The total amount paid out in management bonuses across the group for that fourth quarter performance must have been a staggering amount of money. The necessary group refinancing was done and there is an argument that the end justified the means. The total focus on cash had been essential but should (and could?) have been achievable without having to bribe management across the group to sign up to the programme. In my view the shareholders got a very raw deal.

The results-based bonus programme can create an environment in which some senior managers will focus on what every transaction and every decision is going to do to their bonus. I worked with a CFO who had earned a reputation for calculating, and mentally spending, his bonus on an almost daily basis for the last two or three months of the fiscal year. At one point he had a spreadsheet set up by one of his staff so he could key in the latest forecast for all the key numbers from around the world and the magic cell at the bottom would tell him (to the nearest dollar) how much his bonus was going to be. If our Region was lagging on any of the incentive metrics I would get a phone call to remind me of the potential negative impact on our individual pockets and the demand that I should immediately sort the problem, whatever it may be.

On the same theme, I had a disagreement with my boss at one financial year-end about how some costs should be booked. My boss, it must be said, knew just enough about accounting to be extremely dangerous. Anyway, we were nailed with a bill for £1.2 million associated with remedial installation work on a project that was close to being completed. There was no related revenue and we had not adequately provided for this cost in prior months because our project team had consistently assured us that the final bill would be for a much lower amount. (They also told us that we would probably be able to shift some of the responsibility for the problems that had created the need for the remedial work to another party). When the invoice came in, my boss reviewed the situation with the project team, approved the bill for payment and passed it through to the Finance Department for processing.

With an agreed, billed and approved cost and no related revenue there was no choice other than to book the cost, causing a big dent in the Profit and Loss Account. In full accordance with Sod's Law it was the last month of our financial year and, as you will appreciate, an unexpected dent like this is never a pleasant or popular event. At year-end it goes down like the proverbial lead balloon. In this particular case, what made it more galling was that I believe that the project team had known exactly what was coming but had failed to own up to it and had effectively tried to wish it away (denial syndrome). My boss told me to take the cost out of P&L and put it in inventory. His justification was that the customer's Project Manager had said at a meeting some months before (when responsibility for this work was discussed) that, *if* the whole project was completed on time he would *consider* recommending the payment of a £500,000 contribution towards the remedial costs. The offer was never confirmed in writing and the reality was that the customer's Project Manager had done us absolutely no favours from Day 1 of the project. In my view he had simply dangled a carrot in front of us to get the remedial work started and had no intention of making any contribution towards the cost. I explained the accounting principles, as clearly as I could, to my boss and held firm on my position. Two days later I got a phone call from our President. He started with some flattery and logic - "Come on Ian, you finance guys are smart and you can always find a way to fix these things" and "There's still a lot of commercial negotiation to be done on this project so you could hold the costs back until we see the final outcome". When that didn't get anywhere he cut to the real issue and to the intimidation tactics. "You realise that this mess will hit us all in our pockets. Well, I expect you guys to make your numbers and I'm not going to listen to excuses as to why you didn't. I'm holding you (yes, me!) personally responsible for delivering your Region's forecast profit." I must confess that I had a couple of less than perfect nights of sleep before the CFO stepped in on my side. We took the hit and I was not a popular boy.

Incidentally, picking up on what I said a couple of paragraphs ago, although it is incontrovertible that you only get cash once, I have actually come across a situation where the company's accounting rules for handling securitised Accounts Receivable meant that payment for one invoice could be treated as cash received twice in the same month.

The way it worked was that the receivables were sold to the bank on a rolling monthly basis. The customers continued to settle their accounts direct with the company and the company then passed the monies that they had collected 'on the bank's behalf' to the bank, also on a monthly basis.

In simple terms, what happened was this:

(i) All the qualifying invoices which had been issued in the month of January were 'purchased' by the bank via a single payment to the company in early February (minus the bank's interest and administration charges).

(ii) Netted against the total amount of that payment was the total of the amounts that the company had collected in the month of January against invoices that had been 'purchased' by the bank in January and prior months. (The 'netting' transaction)

> (iii)   This meant that after the initial one-time boost to cash at the outset of the programme, there would be some months when the bank paid us under the netting arrangement and some months when we paid them.

The quirk in this procedure was that, by collecting a January billing from the customer in February and also getting the money for that same invoice from the bank in February, we effectively counted the same cash twice in the month of February. Early in March when we paid the cash over to the bank, via the 'netting transaction', the situation became normalised. (Two receipts minus one payment, equals one receipt).

December was the last month of our financial year and, following one incredibly successful December in terms of customer collections, we went into the new financial year knowing that we had a substantial seven-figure hole (in Sterling!) in our cash flow for the month of January. That was the total of the amounts where we had collected from both the bank and from customers for the same invoices within the month of December and, therefore, the amount that we had taken credit for twice in the same month. Needless to say, the cash-based management bonus pay-outs for that particular year were excellent. Unfortunately all we had done, from the broader business perspective, was to take advantage of a questionable accounting situation and to give ourselves a major headache going into the new financial year. This provides a perfect example of managers exploiting the bonus programme for their own benefit to the detriment of the shareholders.

Many years ago when I was working in the 'pre-PC' computer industry, we used to pay all the staff salaries direct into employee bank accounts but all of our salesmen still received their commissions by cheque. The commission cheques were personally handed over by the Branch Managers at monthly, Friday-afternoon meetings held in the individual Sales Offices. Big cheques were waved in the air or passed around, the successful were praised and the unsuccessful berated. At the same time, salesmen were actively encouraged by their managers to buy bigger and better houses or bigger and better cars and to get loaded up with debt. The company wanted hungry salesmen because hungry salesmen tried harder.

I am mentioning this because I think there is a very important distinction to be made between hungry, in this sense, and greedy. The hungry will try harder which is desirable. The greedy will grab more, which is not. When management greed is packaged along with an entrepreneurial spirit the results can be mind-boggling.

A close friend of mine worked in a major oilfield service business, which had a couple of interesting problems in its IT department.

Firstly they had a Director of IT who had some kind of financial 'arrangement' with their major software supplier that allegedly benefited the Director of IT to the tune of several hundred thousand dollars. Not long after he had been found out, and had left the company, the company embarked on a worldwide ERP implementation.

This implementation did not go well and, part way through the project, a new Project Manager was put in place to try to pull it back on track. Not only did he fail to get the project under control but it transpired that he had managed to set himself up with a couple of nice little side-lines.

With members of the implementation team flying all around the world, a discount deal was established with a well-known hotel group. Our intrepid project leader cut a personal deal with the hotel group. He arranged that, if any individual member of the team booked into one of the group's hotels and didn't claim their privilege club points, then the points would be credited to the project manager's privilege club account.

His second scam was to set up a company with a friend of his and then have all the billings for the contractors working on the project channelled through that company. The boy and his buddy added a cool twenty dollars per hour 'handling fee' to every billing. The project employed fifty or sixty contractors, each working (say) a couple of hundred hours per month. If you do the maths you will find that they had set themselves up with a very nice little earner with the unwitting employer footing the bill. Nice if you can get it!

The fact that this particular company had two of these greedy entrepreneurs in close succession in the same function does raise questions about the company's selection and hiring processes, working environment and internal control mechanisms. On the other hand, maybe they were just unlucky. Given that this money effectively comes out of the shareholders' pockets, I wonder what the shareholders would think if they were made aware of the whole story.

Was this company just unlucky or were there some more fundamental problems at the root of their misfortune?

In similar vein, at one of the company's that I worked for, there was a buyer who was handling the procurement of machined components. His favoured source happened to be a supplier where the owner/manager also owned a travel agency. Until the situation came to light (as a result of an internal investigation) the buyer and his family were enjoying regular free overseas holidays, courtesy of the travel agency. I don't believe that the buyer could have been naive enough to think that the holidays were really free and there is no doubt in my mind that the cost was coming back to us in the prices we were paying for machined components.

While on the subject of greedy employees, I must also mention a couple of Sales Managers in remote locations who I came across. The first was working in Africa and, with a good salary, overseas allowance, area allowance, cost-of-living allowance and a tax equalisation programme. He earned a serious amount of money every month. The company also provided him with a large house and a big four-wheel drive vehicle. With a true entrepreneurial spirit he decided that the house and vehicle were both eminently suitable for running a domestic repair business and he set up a nice little side-line for himself, fixing washing machines and fridges for the expatriate community. Pick-up and delivery in the company's truck was, of course, part of the package that he offered. Staggeringly, when this was brought to the attention of his functional management, they saved his hide because 'he was a good salesman and the customers liked him'. My simplistic view was that he was greedy, under-handed and unethical and that he should have been fired. It was fortunate that he transferred out of our Region shortly afterwards because I certainly didn't trust him any further than I could have thrown him. (And that would not have been far because he was substantially bigger than I was).

The second Sales Manager was based in the Far East. He had apparently told our local agent (a Chinese-Malay) that Head Office was very unhappy with the agent's performance and wanted to move to a different agent. However, he (the Sales Manager) could make sure that this didn't happen in exchange for a slice of the agent's commission. The deal was done and it was an arrangement that stayed in place for a number of years. The company then decided to establish a local manufacturing facility and part of the arrangement was that the local joint venture partner would also be the sales agent. When the incumbent agent was informed of this he wrote to the President of the company claiming that this couldn't happen because his status was protected via his deal with our Sales Manager. The Vice-President of International Sales and I were quickly despatched to the Far East to interview the parties to the problem and get it resolved. The whole sorry story duly unfolded and some weeks later, after due process had been followed, the Sales Manager became a former employee. On a different time-scale the manufacturing joint venture moved forward and the sales agency was moved to the new joint venture partner as planned.

In a similar vein, when I was working in Nigeria, I came across some more employees who had the entrepreneurial self-help spirit. As part of our business, the local company bought and sold a certain amount of used drill-pipe and casing. It wasn't a core activity and the volumes were quite small. We bought the pipe from our oil operator customers when they had no more use for it and sold it to independent water-well drillers or to the construction industry. When one of our expatriate operations managers was on holiday I handled an enquiry from one of the water-well companies and discovered that a couple of our managers were cutting the company out of these deals. They were taking on the role of the middle-man between the oil companies and the water-well drillers in a personal capacity. Profits that should, in my mind, have accrued to the company, and thereby to the shareholders, were going into their individual pockets. When this was reported to our operating management in the US, they came back with, "Second-hand pipe is not really part of our core business, so if these guys want to do some deals on a personal basis, we guess that's okay." My interpretation of the message was, "We hear you but we don't know what to do about it because getting people to go to Nigeria is difficult so we don't want to rock the boat."

However, as Sherron Watkins, the Enron 'whistleblower' succinctly put it, 'Greed breeds more greed' and it wasn't too long before one of our entrepreneurs 'inadvertently' pocketed the cash from the sale of some pipe to a water-well driller, and forgot to give the proceeds to the company, when the pipe actually belonged to the company.

The highly paid leaders of many major companies behave in a manner that sends a message throughout their organisations saying 'greed is okay'. Some leaders actively promote greed as a positive virtue because (erroneously in my view) they equate it with ambition. Over the years there has been a steady stream of well-publicised examples ranging from excessive individually negotiated deals that defied economic reason to actions that were tantamount to monetary rape of the company and its shareholders.

In Chapter 1, I mentioned a couple of specific, high profile examples of excessive management compensation deals that were partially unbundled under the glare of substantial media coverage. Actions that allegedly crossed the boundary from greed and profligacy in companies like Enron, Tyco, WorldCom, and others have actually resulted in criminal charges being brought against members of management.

It's interesting that Sherron Watkins attributed a downward shift in ethical standards at the former Big Five accounting practice, Andersen, to the greed of the partners that, in her words, led them to "start worshipping revenues over technical proficiency".

Greed and Arrogance in tandem can be a real toxic mix. There have been some very public and high profile cases involving so called 'Rogue Traders' and although some of these people were technical specialists rather than managers we can, I believe, reasonably assume that their behaviours reflected the environments that they worked in. Greed related to personal incentive plans and the arrogance to believe that they could beat the markets and the system were almost certainly key drivers in their behaviour. Five of the best known of these (Kerviel, Leeson, Rusnak, Iguchi and Hamanaka) got it spectacularly wrong and cumulatively cost their companies a staggering eight billion pounds. That's eight billion pounds straight out of the shareholders' pockets but the total damage to shareholder value would have been much higher than that. In the case of Barings the bank went under. In the other cases there was reputational damage to the institution and the cost of investigations, internal reviews and systems changes to be added to the direct trading losses. The associated legal and accounting fees will typically be eye-watering and these situations inevitably consume huge amounts of senior management time and effort which would be better spent on more positive activities.

Shareholders should remember that managers who are feeding their own greed are effectively taking cash out of the shareholders' wallets and tucking it into their own.

You wouldn't knowingly sit still while a pickpocket helps himself to your cash, so don't sit still and let your greedy managers do the same thing to you.

Chapter 5: Indecision

Indecision: the state of not being able to decide; uncertainty or hesitation. Also called INDECISIVENESS.

(Chambers 21st Century Dictionary)

An often-quoted saying is that it's better to make ten fast decisions and get seven of them right than it is to spend the same amount of time on one perfect decision or no decisions at all. I subscribe very strongly to this but it does need a couple of major caveats.

a) None of your wrong decisions should be too damaging.

b) None of your wrong decisions should be repeats of previously made mistakes.

There is no mileage in looking for a sympathy vote based on your past successes when you have just made a major league cock-up or made the same mistake for the second or third time. An extreme example of past performance being no excuse for mistakes is the soccer goalkeeper – he can be brilliant week in and week out and then he makes a single error of judgement that costs a critical goal and he is pilloried. Business isn't normally *that* bad, but it can still be quite unforgiving.

Making decisions shouldn't be difficult for any of us because it's something we all do many times every day. We decide when to get up, what to wear, what to have for breakfast, what to do for lunch, which television programme to watch, whether to go to the pub or not, whether to buy something, whether to communicate by phone or e-mail, whether to go to see a film and many, many others. Admittedly in some cases the need to make these day-to-day decisions may have been over-ridden by habit but I challenge every reader to count and see how many actual decisions he makes in the course of a day. The result will surprise you!

Bigger decisions like moving house, changing the car or where to go on holiday obviously require more consideration and care, but most people still manage to make these decisions without too much trauma.

Why then is it so difficult for some managers to make decisions in the workplace?

The answer, I believe, is the simple fear of being wrong.

The fear of being wrong can be driven by a variety of underlying causes including an inherent lack of self-confidence, being in unfamiliar territory, the feeling that you don't have all the essential facts, not wanting to risk a blot on your career copybook and more. You don't have this fear when it comes to your day-to-day decisions because most of the decisions you are making don't have any significant downside to them. What you choose to have for your breakfast isn't likely to have any significant financial downside for your employer or adversely impact somebody else's job! Certainly the consequences of being wrong in the workplace can potentially be damaging for your employer or for the people around you, but that should be no reason for avoiding decisions. In many cases, avoiding a decision can be just as damaging as a wrong one.

If we look again at my definition of management, I think you'll see that it's clear that the manager's role cannot be properly fulfilled without making decisions. Let me remind you....

Managers are people who are employed to strategise, plan, guide, lead and direct the organisation, and to make sure that all the enabling assets and resources are in place, to meet the short and long term goals of the organisation's stakeholders.

You simply cannot guide, lead or direct without making decisions and you cannot ensure that all the enabling assets and resources are in place to do anything without making decisions.

Making decisions is part of the manager's role and if you can't do it, you shouldn't be a manager.

The unfortunate reality is that there are far too many managers out there who struggle to make decisions. There is a smaller, but still significant number, who will do everything that they can possibly do to avoid having to making a decision. It's a sin because every time that a significant decision is delayed or avoided, the failure to act is potentially economically damaging for the business and therefore for the shareholders.

My message for managers is quite simple - don't duck, dive and procrastinate. Assemble the facts, consider the opinions of people who understand the issues, consider the potential outcomes and pull up and shoot. In some situations, you may need to have the added security of a contingency plan but you won't even recognise the need for contingency planning unless you have considered the potential outcomes. Very importantly, you need to understand what it takes to implement your decision. Some of the most costly mistakes in business happen when decisions are made without considering the practicalities and realities of implementation. Mergers and acquisitions, restructuring, re-profiling, expansion, retrenchment and IT projects are all examples of areas where some very expensive mistakes are made as a result of the failure of the decision makers to understand the real difficulties, practicalities and economics of implementation. These are also areas where spin can be a big contributor to failures and this is discussed in Chapter 8. It's all too easy (and very human) to get caught up in the excitement and potential benefits of business projects and overlook the difficulties of implementation. The consultants will tell you about their involvement with past successes and conveniently forget to tell you about the majority of their projects where they struggled. From their perspective, a few rocky patches along the way are an opportunity to sell you additional skills and some more billable days, so a 'bad' project can end up being quite economically lucrative for them. It's amazing the range of issues that can apparently be addressed by hiring in a couple or three experienced 'change managers' to support your team!

When it comes to significant business decisions, another key element in successful decision-making is that there needs to be a clear understanding within the organisation of your decision and the necessity for it. It is obviously best if the decision has the support of the organisation but this will not always be possible. Take, for example, the always-difficult decision to make some employees redundant. It is unlikely that this will ever have broad support across the organisation but the process will be much smoother if the organisation at least understands the reasons behind the decision and why it is necessary in context of the ongoing business. Communication is an essential part of successful decision-making.

Achieving a consensus for decisions among your peers, bosses and direct reports is desirable but the search for a consensus can be a real barrier to decision-making and can also be used very effectively as a tactic for delaying or avoiding a decision.

I had one boss who liked to have a consensus within the senior management team for all major decisions but he did nothing to lead or facilitate the route to consensus. Consequently, we would regularly have management meetings that took nine or ten hours, instead of the three or four hours that they should have taken. We would go round and round in circles while our boss adopted the role of a passive observer. Amazingly, given his lack of participation, he would be raging with frustration at the end of the meeting at our inability to reach a decision. He would then have a one-on-one session with each member of the management team, 'coaching' them in the direction he wanted them to go at the next team meeting so we could get a 'consensus' decision! To compound the problem, his communication skills were not of the best. This guy spoke in half sentences and assumed that people were immediately on the same wavelength as he was. When he asked, "You know what I mean?" or "You understand what I'm saying?" (as he did after every third or fourth half-sentence) most people simply said "Yes" because they didn't want to tell the boss that they couldn't understand what the hell he was on about. Rarely did anyone come out of his office saying, "Well that's clear enough!" There's a funny side to the situation when you look back on it but, from a business perspective, it was a complete shambles and a criminal waste of valuable management time!

In the early nineties we had two similar fabrication facilities for a particular product-line. One was in Holland and the other was in Aberdeen The world market for the particular product was shrinking, we had too much productive capacity and one of the facilities had to go. From a logistical and economic viewpoint, Holland was better placed to cover our served markets in North and West Africa whereas Aberdeen was better placed to cover the North Sea. Logically, economically and intuitively I knew which of the two facilities had to close and I know that my boss had reached the same conclusion. However, in his usual style, he wanted the whole management team to agree. Facility closures are always difficult and, particularly when there is a choice, the real issues can become clouded by strong loyalties and emotions. In this case, each of the vested interest groups had its own compelling set of market projections and a different financial summary to support its particular case. The executioner's blade hung over the neck of Holland, then swung to Aberdeen, back to Holland and back to Aberdeen over a period that must have been close to a couple of years. (A couple of years that, it must be said, seemed more like ten years at the time). Eventually, with the management team apparently unable to reach the 'right' decision, my boss grabbed the responsibility. In a moment of frustration and anger he made the decision that he could and should have made at the outset. We had lost almost two years and spent a lot of valuable management time debating what had really been a non-issue, all in the name of consensus.

By contrast, his successor made an art-form out of letting everyone on the management team have their say, then making the decision that he had always been going to make and portraying it as a consensus. Discussion was focussed. It was cut short if it started to drift and, although everybody had his say, it was in a controlled and 'steered' environment. As a member of the team it was hard to be offended by the process, even when you knew you'd been 'railroaded', because the man did it so well. However, despite this cleverly veiled autocratic approach, I quickly realised that he was also very politically aware and he always took care to ensure that he had canvassed the support of his own boss (and any other influential parties) before diving into any major decisions.

Have you ever noticed the managers who don't have a view until they have seen where the majority are heading? It's only once they have sussed where things are going that they will participate. Then you get something like, "I must say that I agree with Mike and Tom. Transferring the widget business to

Cardiff is something that I have thought for a long time made sense." Yeah, yeah!

I came across a Senior Vice President in a significant business who hated making difficult decisions and who was an expert at 'going with the flow'. I never worked directly for him but I had a good friend who did. My friend said that when you went into this VP's office with a problem that was likely to involve the VP in either confrontation or a decision you could hear all of his orifices crinkling in unison with discomfort. Saying "yes" and giving good news were easy for this VP (as indeed it is for all of us) but he just didn't seem able to get his mouth to form around the word "no" and positively shied away from bad news. On the other hand, he was a very smart individual and a good strategic thinker with excellent customer, industry and product knowledge - okay in a staff or R&D role but hopeless in an operating environment.

A colleague of mine told me that, many years ago when he had been an up-coming staff engineer, this particular VP had been his manager. We'll call the VP 'Fred' for present purposes. At the end of the young staff engineer's annual performance review, Fred asked him "How much of a salary increase do you think you should get?" The young engineer chanced his arm and asked for ten-per-cent. He was amazed to find that was exactly what he received and he has spent the years since regretting that he didn't ask for twenty-per-cent or more.

The worst boss that I can recall having had, from the decision-making aspect, was an engineer and amateur philosopher who liked to follow the decision tree down to the end of its smallest and most remote twig. He would consult everybody who might have a view on the topic at hand and then, wherever possible, he would either pass responsibility for making the decision to the Board or he would make a decision and then ask the Board to endorse it. Funnily enough, most of the decisions that he did make were as a result of his not wanting to have to admit to the Board that an issue was still open and had not been resolved. This individual also had an arrogance that was second to none and an uncanny ability to delegate blame when things went wrong. The fact that he was President of a cross-cultural and high profile Joint Venture Company, where every significant decision was potentially career threatening, probably exacerbated his cumbersome and protracted decision-making process but my guess is that he would have been pretty dire in any environment. As you may imagine, working for him was an extremely frustrating and difficult experience.

My advice to managers and shareholders alike, when it comes to decision-making, is 'beware of he who seeks consensus with religious fervour, beware of he who doesn't have a view until he sees where the majority are heading and beware of the monkey who spends his whole life swinging through the branches of the decision tree.'

Sometimes indecision can be dressed up to look like a decision. The classic example is when things are going badly in the business, there is a decision to reorganise and the reorganisation consists of reshuffling the same pack of people. Many of you will have seen this happening and will know exactly what I am talking about. For me, this kind of reshuffling means, "I have to do something but I don't know what to do, so I'll move some people around." It is a non-decision that buys the head man some survival time but which represents a cost to the business (learning curves, disruption, office moves, knock-on changes, etc.) for which there is unlikely to be any payback. If a football team is losing all its matches, putting the centre forward in the goal, the goalkeeper to left midfield, the left midfielder to right back and the right back to centre forward is unlikely to bring a change of fortune! If your centre forward and goalkeeper aren't performing to expectations you either train them to do better or change them for people who can. Shuffling the positions of the same eleven players isn't going to solve the problem. Business is no different.

Obviously, there are occasions in business when a competent person can struggle and under-perform because he's in the 'wrong' job and, in this case, a change of role is likely to have a positive result. Even footballers have been known to benefit from a change of position but it's a minority case and happens on an individual basis – not across the whole team. To rationalise that the business is doing badly just because there are a number of managers in the wrong jobs, and that shuffling them around will provide a solution, not only defies belief but it begs for the question to be asked, "Who put them into these roles in the first place?" I have actually seen the same cast of characters being reshuffled three and four times in an organisation that was crying out for some real change. Not only is that a sin, it's also a piece of pure, unadulterated and complete nonsense.

So, shareholders, you should be aware that, when you see the same cast of characters being reshuffled for the second or third time, it means you are already overdue for some changes at the top. It is time to go out and find some real decision makers to take care of your company for you.

Chapter 6: Nepotism and Cloning

Nepotism: the practice of favouring one's relations and close friends, especially in making official appointments.

Clone: a person who looks like a replica of someone else.

(Chambers 21st Century Dictionary – abbreviated extract)

In this case, the strict dictionary definition doesn't fully encompass what I am trying to describe but it's as close as I could get in one or two words.

Many managers are comfortable surrounding themselves with people of the same mind-set, cultural background or other characteristics as themselves. For example, some young managers are comfortable leading young teams. Some older managers are comfortable with plenty of grey haired experience in their teams. Some managers who came up through the engineering ranks are comfortable having other engineers around them. The golf mad sales manager may like to have some low handicap golfers in his sales team. The Scotsman may feel comfortable surrounded by some of his countrymen. And so on.

So what's wrong with that?

The answer is nothing, *unless* age, professional background, sporting ability or some other arbitrary attribute is allowed to become more important than the individual's ability to do the job that is required. When that happens, the organisation and its performance are sub-optimised and value for the unknowing shareholders is compromised. Unfortunately, I believe that this happens all too often.

Family favouritism and the 'old school tie' cliques are largely a thing of the past in the developed countries and standardised dress codes and behavioural characteristics are rarely seen in businesses now. However, it's not all that many years ago when employees of companies such as Arthur Andersen and IBM were recognisable by their attire. When I moved to the US in nineteen eighty it was to a $300 million turnover company that was part of a larger quoted group. Despite the size, I found that the lower and middle management ranks of the company contained more than a fair share of members from two inter-married families. It was an environment in which you were always careful to be nice about people in conversation because you were never sure if you might be talking to the mother, sister-in-law or cousin of the person you were talking about. I seem to remember that the Personnel Supervisor and the Payroll Supervisor were husband and wife (or brother and sister or some-such), which is a situation that has to be an auditor's worst nightmare.

However, I think it's fair to say that nepotism and cloning in the strictest sense of the words are no longer the significant problem in the developed countries that they once were.

On the other hand, nepotism is still a major problem in a lot of the developing countries. In most cases it is family or tribally based and the unwary expatriate will probably not even recognise that the problem is there until it bites him in the backside. My direct experience of this was mainly in East and West Africa but I have also seen signs of the same issues in the Middle East and the Asia Pacific region.

During the time I spent in Africa, I found that the biggest sources of friction and dispute in the workplace are family disputes and deep-rooted tribal hatreds. When it comes to hiring new staff or promoting existing staff, the priorities for local managers are easy. Firstly they look to their relatives and secondly they look to members of their own tribe. A third option is rarely needed or entertained. It's quite a while since I lived in Africa but in regular subsequent business and holiday visits, I have seen little evidence of this situation changing. It's particularly difficult for the expatriate manager to get on top of this situation because even once you are alerted to it you still don't know who is related to who unless someone makes it their particular business to tell you. The Equal Opportunities campaigners are certainly going to take a long, long time to crack this particular nut.

In Nigeria the Yoruba staff in our Lagos office and the Ibo staff in our Port Harcourt office missed no opportunity to try to get something over on the other or to try to put them down in front of management. Accusations and finger-pointing aimed at co-workers from a different tribal background were a part of their normal day's work.

Many readers will be aware of, or will have participated in, case studies and practical exercises that demonstrate both the power of synergies and the advantage of having a mix of characteristics and talents within a team. The synergy studies teach us that the team is stronger than the sum of the individuals and it is pretty obvious that a soccer team comprising of eleven forwards, or a cricket team comprising of eleven bowlers, would be unlikely to win anything. In the same way, a management team that has youth but no experience, or one that has experience but which lacks the energy or innovative ideas of youth, will be unlikely to win anything. An essential ingredient for team success is to have a balanced mix of talents and abilities that are put together in an environment where they are actively encouraged to both challenge and feed-off each other. One-dimensional teams don't have this.

Now I am sure that many managers will read the previous paragraph and dismiss it as 'motherhood and apple pie' but, as they do so, I have a question for them.

"If it really is motherhood and apple pie, how is it that so many of you manage to get it wrong?"

And the answer is that we are all human. Every single one of us, from the age of two weeks to ninety-two years (and beyond), likes to be in his own particular comfort zone. As a manager it is very easy to create a comfort zone by surrounding yourself with people who think like you do or who have been brought up through the same career path that you trod yourself. It's a situation that you don't even have to plan or think your way into because your instinct will automatically take you in that direction. The corollary is that it is something that you need to actively think about and plan to prevent if you are going to avoid the pitfall.

Managing diversity and managing confrontation or conflict are both very difficult. Gaining consensus from a multi-cultural team is invariably difficult. Strong-minded and talented individuals will inevitably generate confrontation and conflict within any team. Having a team of like-minded people avoids the difficulties and discomfort so these are compelling reasons for managers to want to remain cocooned in their comfort zone. As evidenced by the sports pages of your daily papers over many, many years, some of the most talented sportspeople are the hardest to manage. Business people are no different.

Managers who can quickly and effectively get consensus from a diverse and strong-minded group are rare. Managers who can channel the energy from confrontation and conflict into solid and united support for the decision that is reached are even rarer.

When you surround yourself with a team of people with which you feel comfortable, rather than with a team of achievers which is more difficult to manage, you are at once making your own life easier and doing your employers a great disservice.

Companies that are predominantly led by one discipline (such as Sales or Engineering) very often have a real problem when it comes to the quality of their management, particularly within the middle ranks. Because smart young people within that key discipline are (rightly) seen as the life-blood of the company, it tends to be the high-achieving salesmen or the technically accomplished engineers who get promoted into management positions. In very many cases, the same characteristics that made them successful in their functional role contribute towards making them poor man-managers and poor leaders. I have worked for a company where the first requirement for someone to be considered for any operational management role was that their background had to be in Sales and I have worked for a different company where the anointed ones all came from Engineering. Both companies had a lot of failures on the lower rungs of the management ladder as people with no natural management ability were promoted into management positions. Both companies also missed out on a lot of latent management talent that existed in other functions. Giving salesmen or engineers an alternative career ladder within their own discipline that doesn't necessarily burden them with a lot of the responsibilities of people management, and thereby avoids future failure costs, can yield some big benefits for the company, the employees and, of course, the shareholders.

In the previous chapter I complained about the reshuffling of people being used as a way of avoiding difficult decisions. In a lot of cases, such reshuffling is directly tied in with this notion that a home must be found for the good engineers or good salesmen. The outset of the problem is when the wrong people are promoted to be managers and start to struggle. From there it gets progressively worse as they get shuffled between different managerial roles as their bosses try to get them into the 'right' job. It's a bad situation but the solution is simple. If they can't manage, they should *not* be managers. It doesn't matter how many patents an individual has registered or how many widgets he sold last year. If he has no aptitude for management, you should keep him in a functional role and leave the managing to people who are good at it. The business will benefit and you'll have a happier and more motivated workforce. Your shareholders deserve no less.

Digressing slightly, I must tell you that I participated in a two-day, off-site team-building exercise some years ago and a young lady from Price Waterhouse (as the firm was then known) came in to conduct a profiling exercise for our management team using Belbin's technique.

As I recall, we weren't particularly well balanced because we had an over-abundance of 'Shapers' and only one 'Completer/Finisher'. However, what really stuck in my mind was that the young lady told us not to worry too much because, as a team, we were reasonably okay. I think this was her politically-correct way of saying that we were not very well balanced but that there were a lot of companies out there who were in much worse shape than we were. She went on to tell us that she had recently finished a similar session at another client where eight out of nine members of their executive team had a primary profile of 'Chairman' and none of the eight had a strong secondary profile. A company led by a team that included eight strong 'Chairman' personalities must have been extremely sub-optimal from the shareholders' view but it must have been a really entertaining place to work!

It must also be recognised that there have been many companies which have achieved outstanding success while keeping control within the family through successive generations. Mars, Lego and Warburtons come immediately to mind together with Baxters Food Group and Glenfiddich Distillery which are both closer to home. These are all companies where the family has had the vision and the sense to bring in the technical and professional resources that have been required to support them and to challenge them as their businesses have grown.

Chapter 7: Profligacy

Profligate: scandalously extravagant

(Chambers 21st Century Dictionary)

Most managers control some level of expenditure out of the company's coffers. Some managers are careful and prudent with the company's money, some are less so and some are simply profligate. The impact on results, and therefore on the shareholders, will obviously be at its worst where a profligate person has direct control over large amounts of expenditure. Every pound, dollar or euro that is improperly or unnecessarily spent is a pound, dollar or euro that isn't available for investment in the business or that doesn't get to the shareholders' pockets via dividends.

A good way of illustrating the point I am trying to make would be for an employee to go to the AGM and pick the attending shareholders' pockets to the tune of, say, one thousand dollars. That, of course, would be simple theft. However, if I spend one thousand dollars of the company's money on something that has no value to the business I may be considered stupid, and my judgement may be questioned, but no one is going to accuse me of theft. If you ignore tax (now there's a pleasant thought!), the result for the shareholders is the same in both cases. So when is a thief not a thief?

Despite all the focus that there has been, and continues to be, on corporate governance and management behaviour, it is always going to be extremely difficult to eliminate profligacy. Prudence or imprudence is to a great degree a matter of personal judgement. There are no clear-cut rules or ethical standards governing this area, so eliminating the worst excesses should be the primary target for prudent managers. The small stuff can be extremely irritating but trying to eradicate it is simply not worth the hassle.

There is actually a school of thought, that I have heard, that says that profligacy in business is not really all that bad because it keeps money circulating and what goes round, comes round. Money spent in bars, restaurants and golf clubs is providing employment opportunities and greasing the wheels of the economy. It's akin to the view that the cost of the Mars exploration programme isn't important because none of the money actualy leaves Earth! My view is that this is utter rubbish. It is a view promoted by profligates for the benefit of profligates and which is unsupported by any logic or common-sense!

During his tenure at Tyco, L. Dennis Kozlowski seems to have been right up among the contenders at the top of the Premier Division in the sport of Profligacy. But please note that, for every Kozlowski in the business community, there are thousands of minor division players competing in the self-same Profligacy League. The amounts involved are smaller but the principle is the same. Across the broad spectrum of global business the amount of money that is unnecessarily or wastefully spent by profligate managers must run into billions and billions of pounds, dollars and euros each and every year.

Shareholders, are you listening?

I always found that a fascinating aspect of reviewing entertainment expenses was to note how closely the type of entertainment aligned with the personal hobbies and preferences of the person doing the entertaining. Logic would say that if I want to show my customer a good time, I would ask him what he would like to do and then arrange something accordingly. Reality, more often than not, is that an employee of the company is using entertainment to fund his own hobby or enjoyment. A quick review of the expenses will soon tell you which of your own staff enjoys the theatre, golf, cricket, hunting, fishing, go-carting, eating-out, eating-in or a night in the pub. This situation is exacerbated because the employee who treats entertaining in this way will, more likely than not, end up mixing with like-minded people in your customer's (or other third party's) organisation. These may or may not be the right targets for the company's expenditures.

I worked beside an American salesman in Africa who spent a lot of the company's money on home entertaining but who rarely had a customer (existing or prospective) in his house. The typical party in his house would consist of friends of his wife, contacts made through the children's school and the half-dozen or so hardened boozers, who exist in every expatriate community, and who manage to tour the party circuit and pickle their livers entirely at someone else's expense. Unsurprisingly, he was not a particularly successful salesman, although he was quite popular within the drinking section of the expatriate community. For this individual 'customer entertainment' meant having an enjoyable social life that was paid for by the company.

By contrast, I worked closely in Africa with a salesmen (also American, as it happens) who was excellent at targeting the key people in the customer's organisation and taking care of them as if they were family, regardless of whether he liked them on a personal basis or not. He wined and dined them at their favourite places, took them to the places where they liked to go and pampered to their likes and preferences even if they were not his own idea of fun. For him, customer entertainment was an essential and important part of his achieving results. Sometimes it was enjoyable for him and sometimes it was a chore, but he always participated with enthusiasm and a smile. Needless to say, he was a very successful salesman.

Certain industries seem to favour particular types of events or forms of entertaining. As an example, the oil business seems to be particularly big on golf, hunting and fishing and the amount of money that the oil industry spends on golf, in particular, for its staff, customers and suppliers must be quite staggering when the oil price is high and the industry is strong. 'Management' meetings at some of the world's top golf courses are extremely popular and some of the bills that result are simply outrageous. The total cost of such an event will typically not only include all the basic necessities like air-fares, car rental, accommodation, food and green fees but it will also include the cost of cart rental, club rental, big booze bills, a tab for all the boys and girls to get their golf shirts and baseball hats at the Pro's shop, visits to the resident beautician and hair-stylist and the provision of some alternative entertainment or excursions for the non-golfers. When the oil price is low and the industry is hurting these excesses are curtailed but they don't go away completely.

The argument put forward to justify this stuff is that it provides a good motivational and team-building session, a chance for people to network and an opportunity to hear the individual and collective views of the company's movers and shakers. Where spouses are also invited, it's to say 'thank you' for all the tolerance and support that they have shown while their partner has been putting in sixty or seventy hours (or more) a week at the office.

What a load of rubbish!

In this day and age, the spouse is either wrapped up in a job of their own or they have a routine at home that gets disrupted if their partner suddenly comes home at five o'clock. Isn't it amazing how senior managers apparently feel the need to acknowledge the role of their managers' spouses but don't feel the need to extend the same hospitality to the wife of the machine operator or welder who is cranking half-a-dozen shifts of ten or eleven hours each in a week. Whoever it was that said that we live in a classless society got it very wrong!

So what should happen?

I would suggest that if team-building is really needed, then get your managers enrolled on a proper team-building course. The ones that I am familiar with usually involve a good helping of physical effort and physical discomfort and are a lot cheaper than Gleneagles, Loch Lomond, La Quinta or Pebble Beach. Make sure that the CEO, CFO and other officers participate as fully as they would have if the golf course had been the venue. As for those long suffering spouses, why not give their over-worked partners a couple of extra days off work so they can go and do something that they want to do as a family. It would certainly be a very human alternative to dragging them away from home to spend time with a bunch of people who they may not even like. If you are genuinely a loving and caring employer you will also include all the people who work excessive hours, and not just the managers. I am sure that Charlie the machinist, big Spike the welder and their respective wives will be most appreciative!

If a group of your management (including the CEO) still love their golf enough to want to play some of the world's most prestigious courses, there is nothing to stop them from putting their hands into their well-filled pockets and paying for it themselves! If they are doing it 'on their own nickel' you can bet that a more cautious style will prevail than when they are doing it on the company's tab. It is amazing to see how the people who are most careless with the company's money are often the ones who are most 'grippy' when it comes to spending their own cash. When the company is paying for managers' playtime and hobbies, events will typically be approached on a 'money's no object' basis. The costs can be huge and the shareholders shouldn't lose sight of the fact that it is their money that is being spent.

Connoisseurs of fine wines and spirits can be expensive managers, particularly if they are in positions where they travel or do a lot of entertaining. I worked with a senior Sales Manager who enjoyed a good drink (quality as well as quantity) and who took some perverse pride in trying to set records for the amount of money that two people could spend on a business lunch. When dealing with him, I often used to wonder whether expensive booze kills off more grey cells than the cheap stuff or whether it was just him!

I remember travelling to the Far East many years ago with our Vice-President, International Sales. An old oilfield hand, he would routinely choose a two hundred dollar bottle of wine for the two of us with our dinner. When I questioned the practice he said, "Young man, I'll tell you exactly what I told the Company President when he questioned my expenses. I don't expect to reduce my standard of living when I travel and if you want to see my grocery and drink receipts from home, to check how I live, I'll be happy to show them to you. Now, what do you think of this particular wine?" I wasn't wholly convinced that he routinely drank that kind of wine at home but it was a good story told with absolute sincerity and I wasn't going to be the one to call his bluff, if indeed it was a bluff.

A point that's often overlooked by the self-appointed connoisseurs of wine and spirits is that, once you are three sheets to the wind, you may as well switch to the cheap plonk because it all starts tasting the same to you at that point. Unfortunately it's once they are three sheets to the wind that the big-spending managers typically start noisily and overtly ordering up the thirty-year old MacAllan Malt Whiskey, the

Hennessey XO Brandy or the most expensive Port in the house. Being seen to know the 'good stuff' seems to be a testosterone thing!

Back in the oilfield boom days, our small International Sales Group (or at least those of the group who were in town) would routinely go out for a Friday lunchtime drink once or twice each month and the bill would inevitably end up as 'customer entertainment' on somebody's expenses. The Vice-President, International Sales would be an attendee if he was in town and he would also approve the Expense Reports. These lunchtime sessions were legendary and I can attest to going into a Mexican Restaurant in Houston with them at midday for 'lunch' and falling (or crawling) out of the restaurant's front door again at eight o'clock in the evening after a 'lunch' that included eight hours of non-stop margueritas and beers. The justification was that the members of the sales team spent a lot of time on the road and in aeroplanes and visited a lot of undesirable locations so it was necessary to allow (or encourage?) them to 'twist off' once in a while as a way of recharging their batteries. (I suppose the modern expression would be to 'chill out'!) Another load of pure, unadulterated bull's droppings! By all means let them 'twist off' or 'chill out' but let them do it in their own time and at their own expense. I must say that although this kind of profligacy was rife in the oil and gas business in the late 1970s and early 1980s I do believe that it has been substantially curbed during the successive painful downturns that the industry has suffered in the intervening years.

Sometimes bad situations can arise without planning or aforethought and a shining example of this was when a group of twenty or thirty people who had been working under a lot of pressure on a major project made their first deliveries ahead of target to the delight of our customer. It was suggested, by the Project Manager, that he should take some of his team to the pub and have a couple of drinks to celebrate their success with the company picking up the tab. This was agreed.

The following morning the office was buzzing with rumours about 'last night's party' and, later in the day, a relatively junior member of the project team came to my office. He rather sheepishly wanted to know what he should do about the four-thousand-pound-plus bill that had been charged to his American Express card the previous evening.

I'm sure that I was never privy to the whole sordid story but it was clear that the 'couple of drinks' had got substantially out of control. Rounds of drinks were apparently being bought at the company's expense for anybody in the pub who was capable of shouting out what they wanted, whole bottles of spirits were purchased and there was a brawl that resulted in some damage to the pub and the police being called. The most galling part for me was the strong and persistent rumour that some of our staff had left the pub carrying bottles of spirits and cases of wine under their arms, which in my view was crossing the boundary from exuberant stupidity and reckless irresponsibility to simple theft. However, it was impossible to pinpoint the guilty and, given the background of their project success, we were reluctant to discipline all the attendees. We drew the disciplinary line at imposing a ban on any such celebrations for the future. The individual who had said 'Yes' when one of the managers asked if anyone had a Gold Card in their wallet was a victim. After we had given him a lot of grief, his Expense Claim was reimbursed in full. However, I guarantee that if he's faced with the same situation again, he won't be the one putting his hand in his pocket to pay!

As I said, earlier in this Chapter, trying to eradicate all of the small incidents of profligacy that occur daily in business would be an impossible task. However, wiping out the big excesses is a more than reasonable goal. Team building sessions, social events and group motivational sessions are all essential to a vibrant and successful business but money spent in this direction has to be directed at getting the maximum benefit for the company rather than at catering for the particular pleasures of a few senior managers.

Shareholders should take it on themselves to ensure that their Board and their senior managers set the right example for the rest of the organisation when it comes to spending the company's money. They should also satisfy themselves that there is a clear understanding throughout the organisation of what constitutes acceptable behaviour in this regard.

Chapter 8: SPIN

Spin: said of information, a news report, etc, especially that of a political nature: a favourable bias.

(Chambers 21st Century Dictionary)

Spin is potentially the most damaging of the seven sins because it involves deception (often deliberate) and is most commonly used in business to hide or underplay bad situations. In the world of politics, it is par for the course to spin information and statistics for public consumption. Opposing political parties can make (and support) wildly different conclusions based on the same set of statistics. They simply choose and embellish the bits that support their case and happily ignore the rest. The SNP in Scotland has turned this into a real art form (or is it a science?). On the other hand, when spin starts in business, the organisation starts lying, or telling half-truths, to itself rather than to the amorphous Joe and Jane Public. When you start deceiving yourself, the consequences can be extremely severe. Everyone knows that politicians twist and stretch the truth to suit their own ends and we treat whatever they say with a healthy amount of scepticism. Put very bluntly, we expect them to lie. However, within a business, I think that managers are entitled to expect nothing less than straightforward honesty from their colleagues. After all (unlike the politicians) they should all be striving towards the same goals.

The sad reality though is that the pressure for results and the big rewards for short-term success are both factors that fuel the fear of failure and the reluctance for anyone to 'fess up' to a bad situation, particularly when it lies within their own sphere of responsibility or influence. The nature of the game is becoming increasingly to make mediocrity sound like excellence and to gloss over anything bad.

In my view spin is a disease of big business. We are working in an era when presentation skills are starting to be valued as much (or more) than technical competence. Honesty and 'telling it like it is' have become devalued commodities. Form triumphs over substance and there is too much smoke, too many mirrors and not enough truth.

I have put together lots of presentations over the years for internal consumption, for higher management tiers and for third parties and I have sat through very many more. I know how easy it is to be selective in your facts, to emphasise the strengths and to downplay (or omit) the weaknesses.

I remember quite vividly an occasion when some of my boss's well-orchestrated spin backfired on him and, more particularly, on me. We had a two-day operational review with our CEO and CFO from across the Atlantic and my boss decided to handle the visit via a series of small meetings where each business unit would present their operational initiatives and action plans in turn, with minimal focus on any financial information. My presence wasn't required at these meetings. On the second afternoon there would be a wrap-up session where I would cover the Regional business and consolidated financials, the projection for the year, major issues and potential upsides and downsides. Although I didn't realise it at the time, the business unit presentations had all been unrelentingly upbeat. They had focussed entirely on specific successes, process improvement initiatives, their plans to aggressively increase market share and upcoming deals. For a day-and-a-half our two visitors had been pumped full of good news – just the way my boss had 'gamed' it.

My presentation was designed to cement the impression that everything was going well but also to ensure that it was understood there were still some significant issues and risks which could jeopardise our financial results. There were only four of us in the meeting room (the CEO, the CFO, my boss and I) and it was all going remarkably well until I put the 'Downsides' slide on to the screen. Our CEO listened to the first two of the eight or nine items that were listed and then lit up all four of his engines and took off.

"Goddammit, I didn't fly three thousand miles to listen to this crap", he yelled. He hurled his pen into his briefcase, zipped the briefcase, stood up and said, "That's it, I've listened to enough of this - I'm out of here!" With that, and a heavy hand on the door, he left.

As you may imagine, there was a long and very pregnant silence in the room before the CFO laughed resignedly and said, "Well, I guess he didn't like that too much. It looks like the meeting is over."

The CEO's behaviour was indefensible. It was a classic mix of rudeness, arrogance and bullying, with a touch of petulance for flavour. In this instance, it was also understandable and, to some extent, deserved. I must confess that I was more upset about the way I had been manoeuvred by my boss than I was about the CEO's reaction. My boss had been far too clever in trying to manage the content of the presentations, he had taken the spin three steps too far and then set me up as the fall-guy at the end. I've made some less than inspiring presentations over the years but that was the only time that my principal audience member actually got up, walked out and slammed the door on the way!

In fact, the CEO strode into my office a couple of hours later. He sat down and said, "We'll reconvene at four o'clock so you can finish your presentation. I am very interested to hear the rest of what you have to say but don't put that crap up again!" Then he got up and walked out. Clearly he didn't see the need for any further explanation or an apology!

Part of spin involves telling people what you think they want to hear and a common manifestation of this in business is in saying that an action or task is completed when it has only been partially addressed.

A classic illustration of this was when, at one of my employers, we had some serious operational and financial problems within our projects business. We were working on a big, high profile project that was running late, on which we had some significant technical and commercial problems and which was burdened with cost over-runs, post-installation rework costs and late delivery penalties. A team was put together to study the bid preparation process, design review procedures and execution processes for that particular project and to come up with some specific recommendations and actions to prevent any future recurrence of the problems. This was a big project and the difficulties we were having were so serious that my boss had to travel overseas to give monthly, face-to-face progress reports to the Chairman of our parent company for quite a considerable number of months.

Processes were mapped, cause-and-effect analyses were carried out and a bunch of recommendations and actions were compiled. Unfortunately, from there, it seemed that the emphasis shifted to doing just enough to label each action as 'complete' so my boss could report that we were making progress and 'get the Chairman off our backs', rather than on ensuring that we were putting robust and resilient fixes in place. As a result, problems were band-aided rather than cured at the root-cause. However, open action items were being closed, the Chairman seemed to be reasonably happy with our progress and the cross-hairs were moving away from between my boss's eyes.

Things then ticked along okay in our Projects business for several years until some of the band-aids started to come unstuck and the same old problems reared their ugly heads again. Some of the key players had changed since the previous round of problems and the new boys on the block didn't recognise the issues as an old story. Needless to say, among the people who *had* been involved previously, nobody was putting up his hand and saying, "We didn't fix it properly last time around."

So, guess what happened! - We started all over again.

Another team was formed, another bout of process mapping was carried out and there was more cause-and-effect analysis. This new effort culminated in a list of recommendations and actions that, for some of us, had a remarkably familiar look to them. Once again, recommendations were reported as implemented and action items were reported as closed but, once again, the fixes were not robust and resilient. In that situation you know that it's only a matter of time before the same drama will have to be played out yet again.

Spin is enemy number one if you want to have a true 'learning' organisation. If you really want to benefit from lessons learned, you have to eradicate the spin.

Acquisitions, flotations, big IT implementations and other major projects are fertile ground for spin. It starts with the zealots who have become emotionally wrapped up in the project, or with the greedy who stand to make a quick buck. The internal selling process will be spun to focus on all the potential benefits and gloss over the myriad of potential pitfalls. Then, once the project is underway, nobody will want to admit that it was based on unrealistic assumptions, that it's falling behind schedule, that unforeseen hurdles have been encountered or that costs are starting to over-run and payback isn't going to be achieved. Reviews and Steering

Committee Meetings will have more spin in them than a spider's web and when senior management eventually realises that all is not well, the point of no return will have been long passed.

How many companies in this kind of situation have ended up saying, "We've spent so much on it already and we're so far into implementation that we have no choice other than to complete it, whatever it takes"? They end up with a sub-optimal, over-priced business unit, ERP system, production facility or whatever, that will never be able to deliver the level of payback that had been expected from it. In many cases, a big factor in taking them past the point of no return is spin.

When I was involved with Six Sigma, one of the ground rules that we set for our projects was that, in assessing payback, we would only consider hard savings that had a direct impact on profit and/or cash. At one point I was asked to review the project assumptions for a project being undertaken in the US and noticed that they were taking 25% (or thereabouts) of any inventory reduction as an annual cost saving. There was a calculation that showed the components making up this total percentage and these included reductions in procurement costs, storage costs and material handling costs.

It was clear that a number of the assumed cost reductions would only be realised if facilities were closed, assets sold or employees made redundant directly in proportion to the inventory reduction.

I queried whether these fell within our rule of counting hard cost savings only and a high profile, e-mail debate began. After a couple of electronic transatlantic barrages, our President interceded with an obviously emotional e-mail that stated, among other things, that "inventory is evil....EVIL" (his block capitals!) and went on to say that the higher number was fine by him if it helped to drive down inventory. This was a clear case of spinning the assumptions to sell the project.

The first problem here was that potential projects were competing for scarce Six Sigma trained resources and the projects showing the fastest payback were the ones being prioritised. The second problem was that the performance of the members of the dedicated Six Sigma group was directly assessed on the actual payback of their individual projects.

A consistent and realistic set of rules for assessing project economics was therefore essential if we, as a management team, were to make sure that we were putting our resources where we would get the best bang for our buck and that we were getting a real return on our investment in the Six Sigma programme. Finance personnel were appointed as the arbiters in the event of interpretational disputes. The whole objective was to make sure that we dealt in hard facts and not in spin. Unfortunately, inventory was one of the President's personal hobby-horses and, in an emotional moment, he apparently forgot the basic objective.

At the same company, we had a young and expanding Supply Management function that was led by an ambitious Vice

President who was a master of spin. To illustrate the success and effectiveness of his team he instigated a monthly summary report of current month and cumulative 'achieved savings', based on latest price versus previous price per part number. The savings shown in this report were very impressive and the third or fourth time that I saw the summary, I asked if these were gross or net savings. The answer was "net". By the end of the year the cumulative 'achieved savings' figure was several million pounds and I was struggling to understand how the benefit didn't seem to be flowing through in our financial results. Either we were passing all the savings on to our customers or there was something inherently wrong with the numbers. I went back to find out exactly how the 'achieved savings' figure was computed and discovered that the reality was that it was a savings only figure. Where the latest price exceeded the previous price on a particular part number, that transaction was simply ignored. The Supply Management Group's interpretation of 'net' was 'net on those part numbers where there is a saving'. By agreeing a price increase with a supplier on one half of his business volume and an equal price decrease on the other half, these guys could achieve nothing but still make themselves look like heroes! This was spin of the worst sort but the Supply Management group presented their figures with absolute, barefaced conviction to any audience that was willing to listen. Fortunately, from a shareholder's perspective, the Supply Management Group's incentive bonuses were based on other criteria.

At risk of repeating myself, I have to say that one thing for me is incontrovertible and non-negotiable and that is that managers need to be honest with each other for the greater good of the whole business.

Here's a short list of 'dos' and 'do nots' for managers to help them in that direction.

1) Whatever your subject may be, try to present a balanced view in internal presentations. Don't gloss over potentially difficult issues because, you never know, somebody in your audience may be able to offer you some input that will benefit both you and the organisation.

2) Don't hide festering problems from senior management. Talk about them. You will probably find that one or more of the senior people have encountered something similar before and can offer you some guidance and assistance. They can't help you if they don't know that you need help. Better still, tell them about the problem and tell them what you are doing to stop it developing into something more serious. I am certainly *not* advocating that you delegate all your problems upwards but senior management has the need and the right to know about potentially bad situations so that they can contingency plan or redirect resources where necessary.

   i. Risk management is about recognising and mitigating risks before they can become issues.

   ii. Don't allow risks to become issues or issues to fester into major problems just because you are scared that asking for help or guidance may be perceived as a sign of weakness or incompetence.

   iii. If you are struggling, ask for help.

3) Don't knowingly oversell something internally, by overstating potential benefits or understating potential difficulties and costs, just because it happens to be a personal hobbyhorse of yours. If you can't sell something honestly within your own organisation, then it's almost certainly *not* a good deal and you shouldn't be promoting it.

4) See things for what they are and not for what you want them to be. Don't lie to your colleagues and, very importantly, don't lie to yourself!

I came across a different, amusing and more politically focussed version of spin when I was working in the Middle East. My employer there was a partly US owned Joint Venture Company and the Arab partners were three politically high profile, State-sponsored investment corporations. One of my duties was to act as the Secretary for the Board Meetings.

After each Board Meeting I would send out a draft set of minutes to the members for comment and correction. What came back was always a bunch of additional verbiage reflecting the things that each of the members had meant to say and the things that with hindsight they thought it would have been politically appropriate for them to have said. The first time that it happened, I went back to one of the Directors and pointed out that some particular dialogue that he wanted included had not actually taken place at the meeting. I very quickly learned that it was my note-taking that was at fault and that the individual member remembered exactly what he had said, word by word! It was clear that it was a debate that I wasn't going to win, even though I happen to know that I am very good at taking minutes, my notes are thorough and I have a good memory for how the meeting flowed and who said what.

Once I had dealt with the external Board members I still had to cross the hurdle of my boss. As the President of the Joint Venture Company and a Board Member he delighted in taking editing licence on the minutes before they were finally released and he had no reticence in presenting things as he thought they should have been said rather than as they were actually said. There were a couple of occasions during my tenure as Secretary to the Board when it seemed that one or two of the individual Board Members and I had clearly sat through two quite different meetings! It was never as dramatic or confrontational as 'black versus white', 'yes versus no' or 'did versus did not', but I certainly learned a lot about how to see things in multiple shades of grey.

To try to eradicate (or substantially reduce) spin the causes have to be understood and eliminated. I believe the causes lie in characteristics that may be inherent in individual employees or that may be conditioned by the culture of the employer organisation (or some combination thereof). The most obvious of the individual characteristics that will drive a person to spin the truth are ruthless ambition, arrogance, self-promotion, self-preservation and a fear of failure. It's a daunting list because all of these can be difficult to identify and all of them will be difficult to change. The bottom line, however, is that internal openness and honesty are key ingredients for a successful and motivated organisation and that spin is like a cancer that will continue to gnaw at the core and fabric of the organisation until it is eradicated.

Chapter 9: The Public Sector Experience

Other than my early career experience in the Training Board, the major part of my direct experience in the public sector was in the Higher Education arena, However, throughout my career and subsequent consulting activities I also gained a lot of insights into the workings of other public sector bodies including Local Councils, Development Organisations, sections of the Foreign Office and a number of Quangos. My observations are based on this broader experience rather than on my direct experience within any one particular area.

What is clear is that six of the seven management sins are alive and thriving in the public sector. The exception, in my experience, is greed. Very few people enter the public sector believing that it will make them rich in monetary terms and management greed is not generally the issue that it is in the commercial world. Some of the MPs who were caught up in the Westminster expenses scandal were undoubtedly greedy but this was an unusual situation and these people were the exception rather than the norm across the broader public sector.

Status, recognition and self-importance are all strong drivers for managers in the public sector and arrogance, indecision, nepotism/cloning and spin abound. The whole structure and way of working is, to my way of thinking, inefficient and therefore profligate but this is more about organisational profligacy than about individual profligacy. Every now and then the media will expose an 'expenses scandal' involving a public sector employee but the excesses are generally of a low level compared with the excesses in big business.

So let me briefly cover the six sins that abound in the public sector.

Arrogance

The arrogance in the public sector is of a different hue from industry and is the arrogance of people who are set in their ways and who do not see the need for change. They have been functioning in an environment where people still believe that they have a job for life and it is an environment that needs a significant shake-up. Every manager in the public sector should be reading, and giving some very serious thought to, John Kotter's book 'Our Iceberg is Melting'.

As Government funding has been and continues to be squeezed, public sector bodies have had to start the painful process of finding ways to do things much more efficiently, finding new income streams and stopping doing things that are unnecessary. Until the inbred arrogance of the senior people in these bodies is shaken out, this will prove to be extremely difficult. Higher Education Institutions for example have recognised the need to develop new income streams. If they cannot find new income streams they are destined to shrink and perhaps disappear. Mergers are likely to be increasingly encouraged by Government with the bigger, stronger Institutions absorbing their weaker local rivals. Many Higher Education Institutions are looking to business as a source for new or increased income streams but most are poorly equipped from a management perspective to make this happen. Shedding some of their arrogance and recognising that behavioural change is essential are gating requirements. Business will not adapt to the Higher Education pace and way of doing things so Higher Education will have to adapt to suit business. From what I have seen this will be a difficult and traumatic journey for many senior Academics.

Academic arrogance has its own unique features and my favourite illustration of arrogance from that environment came from a discussion in a strategy meeting where I suggested that the Institution should be thinking of all its students as paying customers. This generated quite an amount of consternation and debate, which ended with one Professor announcing that, "The students are most certainly not customers. On the contrary, I would say that they are our products". That seemed to close the matter to the satisfaction of everyone who had been involved in the discussion except me. I understand that teachers, tutors and lecturers have a role in the development of students but the arrogance that goes into believing that the students are somehow their product is something that I found quite staggering.

Bullying

Bullying is less overt in the public sector than it is in the cut and thrust of industry but it is inherent in the hierarchical and often quite autocratic management style that pervades in the public sector. A phrase I heard used on a quite regular basis in the public sector was, "You need to tread carefully because you are upsetting the boss". To my way of thinking this was being offered as a threat and a not very subtle attempt at bullying rather than a piece of sage advice.

The status quo in the public sector is all important and non-conformers and change are not welcomed. It is an 'Our Way or No Way' environment although, bizarrely, it would not see itself in that vein.

Indecision

The public sector abounds with Committees and committee structures positively reinforce indecision. Managers who spend a high proportion of their working time moving from one formal meeting to another formal meeting are typically divorced from the day-to-day operations of their organisations. Their knowledge of a subject to be discussed is often gleaned from quickly-read briefing papers, which doesn't help the decision-making process. In a group of twelve attendees at a meeting, it only takes one of them to say, "I think we need some more information before we can make a decision on this matter", and the decision is neatly deferred to a future meeting. Surviving and thriving in this formal meetings environment is an art-form and it was fascinating to see senior people who, when it came to the summation, would always endeavour to be last to comment and then pitch in on the side of the majority. Unfortunately, it is an environment where avoiding decisions is easier than making them and most managers seem to take full advantage of the environment.

Another technique that is used in the public sector to avoid or defer a decision is to hire a consultant to look at the issue or area. This is a double sin because it is profligate indecision. It is argued that getting an independent view is a matter of good governance but that is a poor justification. Consultants are great for helping you to see the woods rather than the trees, to help you focus on the horizon when you are trying to extricate your backside from the crocodile's jaws or to introduce new concepts. What they will not do is to make decisions for you – it is against their culture, their creed and the provisions of their PI insurance! If think you need a consultant to help you make decisions or otherwise help in the day-to-day running of your department, institution or quango then you need to change your managers because that is what you are paying your managers to do.

Having spent the lion's share of my career in industry I found the decision making processes in the public sector to be like death by a thousand cuts. The level of 'backside covering' is way higher than is typically found in industry and that in itself provides a substantial barrier to decision making.

Nepotism and cloning

As you may imagine, where the status quo is all important, nepotism and cloning are alive and well. Managers in the public sector are typically people who have grown and developed within the public sector environment. They work within the system, view any kind of change on an ultra-long-term basis (or not at all) and don't stand up to rock the boat.

When people are recruited from outside they tend to be in this same mould. Fitting in and getting along with everybody are more valued talents than getting results. The sector hires people that it feels comfortable with but, if it is going to change this side of Armageddon, it desperately needs some people in its ranks that will make it feel uncomfortable.

The sector's propensity for recruiting like-minded people is compounded by the public sector salary scales, which are generally too low to attract high-potential staff or experienced high performers away from business, and also by the public sector working environment. People who enjoy the cut-and-thrust of business and who thrive in a dynamic and continuously changing environment will simply die in the polite, structured and one-paced public sector. There has certainly been a significant uplift in the salaries of senior managers across the public sector in recent years and this is particularly the case in Higher Education where the senior management team is typically very well paid. In my view, however, the uplift has been money ill-spent because they have failed to bring in any serious amount of private sector talent or new thinking and they are simply continuing with the same brand of people and mind-sets at the top that they did before but are paying much more for their services.

Profligacy

As I have already said, I think that the problem that exists in the public sector is one of organisational profligacy rather than individual profligacy. Organisation structures and the whole way of working are inefficient and designed to preserve jobs. Demarcation lines are a thing of the past for much of the commercial world but not for the public sector. In the public sector, people still work in silos and they do what they have to do rather than what is required to be done. There is always a willing minority who will actively seek to try to improve things but these folk either get loaded up with work to the point where they are buried or the mainstream will force them to the side-lines. Either way they become ineffective.

Mentioning being forced to the side-lines reminds me of another old story which has nothing directly to do with the public sector but has some analogous relevance to the issue at hand.

In the mid-nineteen seventies I was auditing in a high-volume manufacturing facility. The facility produced electronic and mechanical products and there were a lot of assembly operations where employees were paid on a piece-work basis. I was chatting to one of the assembly workers, who had only been with the company for a few months, and I asked him how he enjoyed it. He told me that it was okay but he wasn't earning as much as he should be earning because he wasn't being allowed to work to his full potential. Apparently, in his first few weeks of employment he had set out to work at what he thought was a good and sustainable rate that would give him a healthy wage packet. When his endeavours were noticed he was escorted to a quiet and dim corner of a storeroom by two of his co-workers and it was explained to him that he was 'messing things up' for all his colleagues. "We work at a steady pace here and we get a reasonable income. We don't have to bust a gut and we don't like outsiders coming in and screwing things up for us. Slow down or something very bad will happen to you". The message was clear and he heeded it.

They don't take you out behind the bike-sheds for a beating in the public sector but there is unquestionably an inbuilt institutional pressure for conformity that achieves the same net effect. It was interesting to see how much of what I regard as inefficiency in the public sector was defended internally as being essential for 'good governance'. In my view, good governance should be about ensuring that Joe Taxpayer is getting the best bang for his buck across the whole length and breadth of the public sector and that is going to entail some massive changes in structures, processes and behaviours. It is going to be hugely difficult but I am an optimist and I believe that the day *will* come.

Spin

'Form over Substance' could be the public sector's motto and here you will find some real professional spinners. Tony Blair's Government demonstrated public sector spin at work in a very visible way but it thrives at every level of the public sector.

It probably sounds like motherhood and apple pie, but the first step in solving any problem is to recognise that the problem exists. The second step is to understand the problem and the root cause. The third step is to fix it at the root.

Because it has zero tolerance for bad news, the public sector rarely manages to take the first step. "We have a no blame culture here" would be more accurately stated as "We cannot say something is wrong in case we have to attribute blame". Little successes are presented as major triumphs and bad things never happen. When bad news does have to be faced, there will be a formal investigation (in the name of good governance) and a report will follow so long after the event that everyone has forgotten what the problem was. This is not a recipe for achieving solutions.

When the new Holyrood Parliament was built with a budget over-spend of more than one thousand per-cent it justifiably grabbed the headlines. It offers a classic case study in how *not* to run a project and the subsequent Public Enquiry exposed a lot of reality-denial and a lot of spin. We learned that there was no locking-down of a clear functional specification or agreed detailed design at an early stage. Accountability and responsibility were delightfully vague throughout the project and commercially the contract was a stinker. Real numbers were either unavailable or were suppressed and the public didn't become privy to the full scale of the problem until very late in the day.

How can this happen? The answer is reality denial, backside covering and a healthy dose of spin. Regrettably these seem to be genetic disorders throughout the public sector!

Chapter 10: Conclusion

With an ever-increasing focus on corporate governance issues, more stringent reporting requirements and greater penalties for managers who 'cross the line', the interests of shareholders have never been better protected.

Or have they?

Much of what is being put in place is concerned with the niceties of corporate governance, the proper assessment of business risks and stricter compliance with reporting, regulatory and legal requirements. Internal Audit departments are being expanded, a new breed of Risk and Compliance Manager has been created and all this new business that has fallen into their laps must have the risk consultants and audit firms thinking that every day is their birthday.

It has been an interesting cycle for the audit firms over the past twenty years or so. Back in the sixties (and earlier) the audit took as long as the auditor thought he needed to satisfy himself that the numbers he was auditing were okay and, more often than not, the audit fee went up each year at least in line with inflation. Much of the grunt work in those days was carried out by inexpensive 'Articled Clerks', changing your auditor was relatively difficult and the audit profession was a very comfortable place to be. Then companies started to wise-up to the fact that audit fees were like any other cost. They could be negotiated or even put out to tender. The era of the lowly-paid 'Articled Clerk' was passed (sadly too late for me) and the starting salaries for graduates entering the profession moved inexorably upwards. The world of auditing became a much more cut-throat place. Competition for clients and for staff had become a much bigger part of the audit firms' daily lives. At first, the inflationary fee increases were no longer automatic and then fees actually started to be driven downwards. More and more companies put their audit work out to tender and the audit profession was no longer the comfortable, secure place that it had once been. Mergers between audit firms became the order of the day and audit staffs were trimmed. The audit firms increasingly looked to consulting and other services to supplement their now not-so-lucrative audit business.

One global engineering group put their worldwide audit out to tender. At the end of the process they selected three 'globally approved audit firms' and then allowed individual Country Management to select one of the three. In many countries this led to a further round of tendering in which a few more pennies were rung out of the hapless auditors. With most things in this life, you get what you are prepared to pay for and the depth and quality of your statutory audit is no exception. Yes, the audit firms have standards that they have to conform to, but the need to reduce the number of man-hours on each audit was unquestionably a significant driver in the move away from detailed checking to a higher level of 'process and internal control review' type of auditing. Materiality levels went up and scope reduction was the order of the day.

At the same time as changes were taking place in the economics of the audit firms, the business of their clients was becoming ever more complex. Almost inevitably, auditing standards slipped. A few well-publicised disasters, a piece of draconian knee-jerk legislation and suddenly auditing was back to the fore. The audit firms are now more securely back in the driving seat on both scope and fees than they have been for many years. As an old boss of mine used to say, "What goes round, comes round."

The Sarbanes-Oxley Act, which was passed in the US in the wake of Enron, World-Com and other such fiascos, set off a paper chase of almost unprecedented proportions covering (in broad categories):

- Corporate Governance and the Audit Committee
- Certification, disclosure and Internal Controls
- Financial Statement Reporting
- Executive Reporting and Conduct

There is no doubt that getting a 'high risk' rating at the end of a 'Sarbanes-Oxley Compliance Review' carried out by your external auditors is going to mean a more stringent audit. A more stringent audit means more time and more time means more cost. Management that is now faced with the very real threat of long jail terms and/or big fines is no longer playing hardball with the external auditors.

What seems to be missing in the new legislation or regulations is anything really substantive covering the softer areas of management behaviour addressed in this book. The reason is probably the simple one that it would be almost impossible to legislate or regulate meaningfully in this area.

So, all you shareholders out there, what are you going to do?

Here are some suggestions

➢ Make sure you have the right balance of talents and characteristics for managing the business on your Board of Directors.

➢ Make sure that the Board Members understand the requirement to have balanced talents and characteristics at all levels of management in the business.

➢ Make sure that all your Non-Executive Directors understand the business and can add real value to it.

➢ Give a broader role to knowledgeable and effective Non-Executive Directors.

➢ Have a Remuneration Committee with real teeth.

➢ Put the softer aspects of management behaviour on the agenda for both your internal and external auditors. This will have a cost but the payback could be huge.

Many Boards of Directors of larger companies comprise of a few executive directors and some non-executive directors who are appointed for their name or their perceived influence rather than for their knowledge of the business or their management abilities. Non-execs from different backgrounds always look good on the letterhead and in the Annual Report. A well-known banker, someone with a political background, a couple of heavy-hitters from your own industry, a couple of prominent names from other industries and a token academic would be fairly typical for the non-exec side of the Board. Obviously, if a couple of them can be ethnic minorities and/or women this is even better! The executive directors provide the dual function of running the company and managing the interface with the non-execs. Apart from passing resolutions and participating on Board committees, the non-execs are, in too many cases, divorced from the real management of the Company. From the shareholders perspective they should expect the Board of Directors to be responsible for the management of the company and they shouldn't give houseroom to any Directors who aren't capable of fulfilling, or significantly contributing to, that function. That means the non-execs as well as the executive directors.

The Board needs to be balanced in terms of its members' experience, abilities and characteristics. Why not have psychometric profiles of the Directors taken once in a while and made available to the shareholders? Wouldn't you as a shareholder like to know if the Chairman of a company in which you are an investor is standing two steps to the right of Attila the Hun or if the non-execs are a bunch of 'yes men'?

Shareholders need to take a much more aggressive interest in who is on the Board, why they are there and how much they're paid. If you are not happy with what you see, start to make a noise about it. You may be surprised at how quickly and how loudly other dissenting voices will join in!

Once you're happy with your Board, make sure that the members all understand your requirement for having balanced abilities and characteristics within management peer groups at all levels in the organisation.

The suggestion that non-executive directors should have a broader role is by no means ground-breaking. However, we would go beyond the usual menu of more participation on board committees or a bigger role in decision-making. I would make it a requirement that non-execs visit the company's major facilities and meet informally with local management on a regular (quarterly), rotational basis in order to help them understand what makes the business tick. It will also help them to understand whether there is the right mix and quality of management throughout the business. If they can't meet this commitment and contribute positively to the business while doing it, they shouldn't be on the Board. Hoof them off and find yourselves somebody who can.

Once the non-execs have an adequate understanding of the business, they should be in the majority on a Remuneration Committee that approves executive salaries and *all* management incentive programmes. Incumbent on the Remuneration Committee will be ensuring that the company isn't paying packages that are above market rate as a reward for mediocre performance at any level in the organisation.

Both internal and external audit departments are in the unique position of being exposed to the organisation and its employees in the workplace for extended periods of time. As a routine matter at the end of each audit they should summarise their observations regarding local management's style, the apparent motivation levels in the organisation and any soft-issue concerns that they may have, which would *not* normally be part of their audit report. They should then present a summary of their observations to the Board of Directors on a regular basis.

All the operating folk out there will cry in unison, "What the hell do the auditors know about the business?" The answer is actually "More than you give them credit for". However, the fundamentally important point is that they don't need to know a lot about the business to do what I am suggesting. The auditors see a lot of different sites and different businesses and they should certainly be able to differentiate between a happy, motivated, well-run team and a depressed, de-motivated, disorganised group of people. Their reports would only be 'one man's' opinion but they could serve as a very useful early warning to the Board of some potentially bad and damaging situations.

Another area on which the auditors could be specifically asked to comment would be the reasonableness (or otherwise) of the level of costs incurred on travel, entertainment, company sponsored events and management 'perks'. If there is a travel policy in place that the auditors feel is over-generous they should be prepared to comment on it and not simply accept it because it's the approved policy. The auditors should never forget that management sets the policies but the shareholders own the business! Just because the CEO has approved all the bills for his wife's birthday party doesn't make it an acceptable corporate event! These reports on the reasonableness, or otherwise, of certain specific expenses would also be somewhat subjective but they may help to stop bad practice at a low level.

As a final message to shareholders, I would say this.

Remember that it's your business. You (through the business) pay the directors and managers to run the business on your behalf and to keep your best interests at the forefront of their thinking at all times. The business is not there for the benefit of the directors and managers. You need to understand the type of management that you have and, if you are not happy with it, do something about changing it. The Board of Directors can either be your interface with the business or it can be a barrier between you and the business. If you suspect the latter, it's time for a change.

It can be difficult as a small shareholder to make your voice heard but, if you don't make a noise, nobody will hear you. Go to the AGM and make your points, or find a shareholders' forum through which to make your views known. One small shareholder telling the directors that they are falling short of expectations isn't going to persuade them to change their behaviour or to sack themselves, so you have to find other routes.

Shareholder power does manifest itself from time-to-time and there have been some high-profile examples. The shareholders at Glaxo rejected the Chairman's proposed pay package, the shareholders at ITV forced their Chairman to step down from the Board and the shareholders at Sainsbury's blocked the appointment of a Chairman who didn't meet with their approval. The Chairman of Shell stood down after a campaign by dis-satisfied shareholders and it was the shareholders at Disney who unseated Mr Eisner.

Obviously it's easier for shareholders to force issues at the Board level than it is for them to exert influence deeper into the organisation but they need to use the Board to actively address any concerns that they may have about how the whole organisation is functioning and performing.

If you are going to have non-executive directors, make sure that they add real value. If they don't, you don't need them. If they don't have a deep understanding of the business, its major processes, its markets and its competitors then it's hard to see how they can really be adding value. The non-exec members of your Board who are drawing their fees in return for the privilege of using their name are not going to bail out the company when it is filling up with water from multiple leaks in the lower tiers. You certainly need Board members with vision, creativity and connections but make sure that they have a practical side too. If your Board needs theoretical or ethereal input, there are plenty of business books that the Board members can read and I can certainly recommend at least one! Give the non-value-adding non-execs the Ann Robinson treatment and bid them "goodbye".

Use your auditors more effectively. Special reports of an 'observation and opinion' nature shouldn't cost a lot of money and can give you some useful insights into your business.

The new legislation that is designed to protect your interests as shareholders is going to cost you a bucket load of money in compliance expenses. Unfortunately, you don't get a say in this and you will find that, faced with potentially outrageous personal penalties, your management is sparing nothing to ensure that they have a paper mountain and a million procedures in place to cover their backsides and keep them out of the poky. It is also likely that much of this will be 'window dressing' and beneath the written policies and procedures life will go on at the coal-face in the same way that it always has. Eliminating the gap between 'how it should happen' and 'how it actually happens' is a major on-going challenge for all businesses.

The people you are relying on to protect your interests are your directors and managers and the only way that you can be sure that your investment is being properly nurtured is to become more interested and involved in knowing how your company is being managed and by who.

If you find you have 'sinners' in your congregation you should be sending them to join another church as a matter of priority.

APPENDIX 1 – THE NUMBERS GAME

In Chapter 4, I mentioned that 'appropriate financial engineering or finagling' might be used by managers to try to avoid reporting results that exceeded those required to earn them their maximum bonus. The fact is that this is only one of many situations in which financial results are likely to be manipulated and I thought it might be worth elaborating a little on the broader topic of how and why and how this happens

'Results management' has been around in business for a long, long time and most successful managers do it. One major reason is that investors and analysts like to see progressive positive growth in all of a company's key metrics. Orders, order backlog, revenues, operating margins, profit and cash flow are all expected to increase steadily and progressively from year-to-year. Big swings in performance make investors nervous. Nice steady improvements in all the key performance indicators make them comfortable and, as we all know, management likes to make the investors comfortable!

As a consequence, trying to take the spikes out of performance, and keep reported results steady and progressive, has developed as a management skill. As an example, let's say that Company A's target (and its investors' expectation) is for a six-per-cent growth in new orders. If the company can deliver a six-and-a-half-per-cent increase and defer a couple of big orders to get a good start to the next fiscal year, why not do it?

When the company is successful and results are good, it is easy to be a little conservative with the numbers. Auditors rarely take exception to a company erring on the side of caution although changes in accounting standards have stopped some of the excessive provision taking and manipulation that went on in the past.

The other side of the coin is that, when companies are not so successful, managers can be tempted to try to anticipate positive events in their results and to defer bad news. More often than not, this becomes the slippery slope to hell, because robbing Peter to pay Paul (or next year for this) is never a successful strategy. It is rather like standing at the bottom of a pit and trying to dig your way out – the harder you shovel, the deeper you go. Many, if not most, of the high profile corporate failures over recent years have had their roots in this kind of situation. Driven by a mixture of their own arrogance, greed and indecision, managers will first resort to spin and then to more flagrant cheating and deception in order to try to preserve their position and their income. By the time the problem becomes public, it is too late to do anything about it.

Tesco in the UK and Weatherford in the US have been recent examples where financial results have been significantly mis-stated.

Despite all the regulatory changes that are designed to protect shareholders, this problem will not go away until a business environment is created where the time is taken to understand (if not tolerate) failure. The suppression of bad news has to stop and, at the same time, management's arrogance, greed and spin have to be brought under control. Bad business situations and poor managers are very much like a cancer – identify them early and you have the chance of making a successful cure. Allow them to remain hidden for too long and you are past the point of no return.

This is a fundamental issue for shareholders to grasp because, when the company goes under, it is they (and not the managers) who stand to lose the most.

Let's explore some specific (and common) issues, starting at the front end with orders and working our way through to cash-flow.

Orders and Order Backlog

The rate of order intake indicates whether a business is growing, static or shrinking and the order backlog presents future revenues. It follows that order intake and order backlog are important numbers for managers and investors alike. So what constitutes a bookable order?

An order must have certain attributes before it is booked. For a start, it should be definite, unconditional and of known monetary value.

Deferring the booking of a new order is quite easy. You simply put it in a drawer for a week, or a month or whatever, and say that it's 'pending clarification of one or two points'. Provided that this doesn't mess up production scheduling or jeopardise the required delivery date, no harm is done.

Pulling bookings forward is not normally possible. Instead, what happens is that instruments that are not really orders are treated as orders to keep the bookings figures up.

A Letter of Intent from a customer is usually no more than that. It will typically be contingent on certain events and will often be non-specific in terms of value. Nonetheless, in times of need, some companies will treat a Letter of Intent as a bookable order.

If a customer gives you a three-year order for supplies or services, worth £100,000 per year but renewable annually, what is the value of that order? Clearly it is £100,000 because the annual renewal provision makes the first year the only part of the order that is definite. However, pressure on orders might cause some companies to 'take a chance' and book this one as £300,000.

Similarly, there are managers who will put an estimated value on an open fixed-term (time-wise) stocking or supply contract where they have no guarantee of any call-offs or deliveries. (The more normal approach is to record each call-off or each supply as an order at the time that the customer gives his instruction). I mentioned in Chapter 4 that, at one of the companies I worked for, it was intimated that orders might become one of the criteria on which management bonuses were based. Interestingly enough, the CFO immediately asked me to put a booking value on all our stocking contracts "in case we need to treat them as orders". Fortunately, as it transpired, orders were not made part of the incentive plan. The issue faded away and I was saved from one of those battles that you know you have to fight but you know you are going to lose. I fundamentally disagreed with the notion that these were bookable orders but, if push had come to shove, and with management incentive payments at stake, my views would have had little value.

Revenues

In Europe and the US, there are some well-developed principles and regulations governing revenue recognition and it's an area that the external auditors take a strong interest in. Nonetheless, there are still ways in which management can play with the numbers.

Deferring revenues can be as simple as delaying the shipment of a product or the provision of a service. Obviously there are the customer's wishes and requirements to consider, but pushing revenue out from one accounting period and into another is usually quite straightforward. Artificially pulling revenues forward is much more difficult but by no means impossible.

In the nineteen seventies I worked for a computer company that prided itself in having a five year growth record which, in percentage terms, on a year-on-year basis, was better than that achieved by IBM during the same period. At that time, IBM was very substantially the worldwide EDP market leader and was viewed with almost iconic reverence as a successful and well-managed company. To illustrate how important it was to be seen to outperform 'Big Blue', the company used to go through hoops at the end of every fiscal year to ensure that its Annual Report could be issued and dated one day earlier than IBM's Annual Report. This, it was believed, sent the message to the business world and to the investors that the company's financial operations were more efficient and effective than those of IBM. Obviously a company that can publish its Annual Report in a matter of weeks after its fiscal year-end is an efficient, disciplined and well-managed outfit! In fact, the company was so efficient and effective that, although the company's fiscal year-end was December 31st, all its non-US operations really had an effective year-end of November 30th. That was the only way that it could ensure that the Annual Report publication deadline was met!

When the company's revenues looked as if they were heading for a year-on-year fall, it announced a change to its revenue recognition policy. The pre-existing policy was broadly that revenue was recognised when a unit was shipped to the customer. The replacement policy was that revenue could be recognised on all units that were completed and tested and which were only waiting for packaging prior to dispatch. The policy change was announced just a few weeks before the fiscal year-end and the one-time pick-up that came from the change was enough to ensure that the corporation's revenues showed a small year-on-year growth, albeit on a slightly uneven playing field.

Another accounting policy change, that I have seen used, which gives a one-time boost to revenue, is to change from a shipments based revenue recognition policy to a 'percentage of completion' (PoC) policy for long-term contracts. This one has an additional benefit because there can be quite a lot of flexibility in defining what constitutes a long-term contract. The motivator for this change in one case was not so much to increase revenue but rather to get the associated increase in operating margin and net profit to achieve targeted results and (you guessed it!) to secure higher management bonuses. The internal policy was changed so that 'major' contracts would be accounted for under the PoC rules. For this purpose, a major contract was defined as any contract that had a scheduled life of more than twelve months from receipt of order to final delivery and a value of more than one million dollars. In a seven-hundred million dollar business, with regular straightforward product orders exceeding one-million dollars, this monetary threshold was ludicrously low. As often happens, the policy change was rushed into place with a target number in mind and the objective was a barrier to common-sense and rational thought. Within two years, the monetary threshold was pumped up to a more sensible level.

Operating Margin and Net Profit

Not so many years ago it was relatively easy to smooth the flow of reported profits by deferring profits from strong trading periods and then recognising them in weaker trading periods via the use of some innovative provisions and reserves. These days it has become much more difficult due to the introduction of restrictions on the use of general provisions and reserves.

During the halcyon days of the oil-boom in the late nineteen-seventies and (very) early nineteen-eighties we typically carried the equivalent of four to six months of pre-tax profit on the Balance Sheet, in the form of excess provisions and reserves. This may sound like a lot but, in a deeply cyclical industry when a downturn hits, those excess reserves were burned up in next-to-no-time. If operational management could react quickly to changing circumstances and adjust the business accordingly, these provisions and reserves would 'buy' them a few months to make their sizing adjustments and prevent the financial results from going down the toilet. If they failed to react, it just meant that the numbers collapsed three or four months later than they otherwise would have and the CEO and CFO enjoyed three or four extra months of employment.

I remember a colleague and myself sitting late one evening, in the office of the company's President in Houston, being very forcibly told by the President of the company that the month-end figures must be wrong because a one million dollar loss for the month was simply impossible. The President told his bean-counters, in very clear terms, that the numbers could not be reported to the Group headquarters because they were so obviously flawed. The bean-counters told the President that they had no choice other than to report the figures. The President said, "No". For a while the three all gazed out of the window hoping for some kind of divine intervention to solve the impasse. The sad truth was that the company had been losing the same amount of money in each of the previous four or five months and the President knew it all too well. However, in the previous months the bean-counters had been able to 'dip in' to the cookie-jars and report modest monthly profits, which should have bought time for some remedial actions to be put in place. Instead of using that period to adjust the business, the President had put his head in the sand and hoped that the market would pick-up and bail him out. Reality was that the market had gone into a deep and long-lasting trough, the cookie-jars were empty and there was no quick way to stop the bleeding.

Eventually the three parties compromised by agreeing that they should instigate some limited checking of the numbers and delay the release of the results by one day, to allow the President time to 'warm the water' with his boss. The CFO would call Group HQ and tell them that the results would be a day late.

It was galling to find that the President had made no attempt to make his boss aware of our true business situation at any time in the previous five months. This could have been reality denial or simple fear for his job – either way his indecision had made an already bad situation much worse. As expected, the checking of the numbers didn't reveal any significant errors and they were submitted to Group HQ one day late as promised. It wasn't too many evenings later that the President was looking for a new employer.

Although it's not of particular relevance to this book, it's interesting to note that during the oil industry collapse in the early-to-mid nineteen eighties a number of major oil service companies incurred restructuring charges that wiped out four, five or even six years' worth of the profits that they had made during the preceding boom period. From a shareholder's perspective, that is a staggering statistic. Rarely has an industry been caught out so badly and with its underwear so firmly entangled around its ankles.

When the downturn came, many of the oil service companies were right in the middle of major facilities expansion programmes that they were convinced would be needed to support an ever-growing market. Many of these new facilities became redundant before they were even completed and many existing facilities were no longer required. The industry switched from expansion mode to deep retrenchment in a matter of five or six months. My employer at the time had a closing order book of over $300 million at the end of one fiscal year in the early nineteen-eighties and more than $100 million of this was cancelled in the first quarter of the following year. The major customers made it very clear that 'in the interest of future business' they didn't expect any demands for cancellation charges. The companies that reacted more slowly to this dramatic change in the market (and there were many of them) could be recognised by the greater magnitude of their losses over the next few years.

To compound the market change, the oil operating companies had over-ordered essential equipment during the boom period running up to the bust, to try to protect themselves from the operating limitations caused by a capacity-constrained supply chain. This meant that, not only did the service companies see orders cancelled and new orders drying up but they were faced with the prospect of the operators having to deplete their own stocks of equipment before any significant new orders started to flow. For the supply chain, this so called 'customer inventory overhang' was a bit like being given a solid kick in the privates after we were already on our knees in the dirt. Rental tool companies and rig operators who had been building equipment for a continuing boom suddenly found themselves with piles of expensive assets sitting around in yards and warehouses gathering dirt and rust. Financially it was a real mess.

The more recent drop in the oil price from over $100 to around $40 has been devastating but the older folk in the industry have lived through it all before.

There is perhaps an interesting parallel to be drawn with the 2008 banking collapse. Comparing the before and after behaviours and the long term ramifications for the two industries would be a hugely interesting exercise but one which would merit a book in its own right.

Anyway, this is another digression from the topic, so back to the book.....

Another useful way of finding some one-time profit is to sell surplus or under-utilised assets for above their net book value. In an ideal world management should be focussed on this kind of opportunity on a continuing basis. Unfortunately it's more likely that, under the everyday pressures of business life, they will only look for this type of opportunity when their business is struggling.

Cash

I have written quite extensively about cash in Chapter 4 and it is certainly the easiest of the key financial items to influence.

In general, those of your customers or suppliers who are not as cash-focussed as you are, will always entertain deals that offer them a meaningful economic advantage versus their own cost of borrowing or versus the income that they are earning on deposits or investments. All that is necessary is to agree a level of compensation for the time/cost of money that makes sense to both parties.

If you want to improve your cash position and you are not concerned about the P&L impact of what you are doing (in terms of the interest cost), or about your reputation in the marketplace, then there are lots of opportunities for you.

o Offer favourable deals to individual customers for early invoice settlement.

o Factor or securitise your Accounts Receivable.

o Stretch your Accounts Payable to the limit.

o Offer individual deals to suppliers to pay them interest in return for deferred payment terms.

- o Enter into 'Sale-and-Lease-Back' deals on assets. Property is the asset that is most commonly utilised in this way. However, any asset that has a clearly definable stand-alone market value and a (reasonably) readily available market is likely to be considered by the financial institutions for this kind of deal. The cost will reflect the level of risk inherent in the transaction for the particular financial institution but this component is usually small because typically they will not do deals that involve any significant commercial risk for themselves!

- o 'Fire sale' your surplus or redundant assets.

- o Offer pricing discounts in return for progress payments from customers on major contracts.

- o Offer bank guarantees in place of contractual cash retentions by customers covering the warranty periods of major contracts.

The concept of wanting to delay the receipt of cash will be totally alien to most people but, as has been previously described, the structure of some incentive programmes may actually encourage managers to want to defer cash from one accounting period to another. Of all the financial finagling, this (as you can well imagine) is the easiest to achieve. The actions that can be taken include.......

- o Pay your creditors early. Very few of your creditors will object to being paid early and it is very likely that some of them will be prepared to give you some generous discounts for early payment. When you are managing cash right through to the last day of an accounting period or the last day of your fiscal year, bank transfers can be used to get cash off your Balance Sheet until quite late in the last day. I have seen me sending the Cashier to the bank at 2:00 pm on December 31st with a bunch of manually prepared 'CHAPS' transfer forms for same day processing to 'get rid of' cash that had been unexpectedly received earlier that same day.

o Offer deferred payment terms to customers who you know have some cash-flow difficulties.

o Accelerate capital expenditure programmes.

A final thought

That two plus two equals four is incontrovertible. However, if you have two and two and a smart Controller, Finance Director or CFO then the answer can be presented as something less than four or possibly something more than four within any one accounting period. The important thing for managers to remember, and shareholders to note, is that the Finance Director's smoke and mirrors are never more than a matter of timing and eventually the truth will out. In the long run, two and two will inevitably prove to equal four.